The

SECOND COMING

The SECOND COMING

SIGNS OF
CHRIST'S RETURN
AND THE
END OF THE AGE

JOHN MACARTHUR

CROSSWAY BOOKS
WHEATON, ILLINOIS

Cover design: Josh Dennis

Cover photo: Getty Images

First printing, 1999

First trade paperback edition, 2003

Printed in the United States of America

Library of Congress Cataloging-in-Publication Data

MacArthur, John 1939-
    The Second Coming : signs of Christ's return and the end of the age /
John F. MacArthur.
      p. cm.
    Includes bibliographical references and index.
    ISBN 13: 978-1-58134-757-9
    ISBN 10: 1-58134-757-X (alk. paper)
    1. Eschatology. I. Title.
BT821.2.M23 1999
236'.9—dc21   99-30666

VP		18	17	16	15	14	13	12	11	10		
18	17	16	15	14	13	12	11	10	9	8	7	

To Clarrie and Edna Pearson,

beloved friends and faithful partners in my ministry for many years. Though we are separated geographically by half a world, we stand together looking for the blessed hope and glorious appearing of our great God and Savior Jesus Christ.

Contents

INTRODUCTION

I believe Christ will literally return victoriously to earth one day in bodily, visible form. My convictions on this point are as emphatic as my belief in Christ Himself. My faith in the future return of Christ is as firm as my certainty about past redemptive history. Furthermore, I would argue that the *fact* of the Second Coming is a cardinal doctrine of Christianity. It is the end and goal of God's purpose on earth, and the divine climax will be as precise and purposeful as every other revelation of God. Those who abandon the hope of Christ's bodily return have in effect abandoned true Christianity.

THE DANGER OF DENYING THE SECOND COMING

This is a vital issue today. More and more people who want to call themselves Christians are disavowing any expectation of the Second Coming. For example, liberal theologians long ago gave up their belief in the literal return of Christ. Some of them simply spiritualize all the prophetic Scriptures, claiming the only "Second Coming" of Christ occurs as He is received into individual hearts. Others go even further, treating the apostles' hope of Christ's return as a myth and a false expectation—essentially rejecting the biblical promise of the Second Coming and taking their place with the scoffers (cf. 2 Pet. 3:3-4). And that kind of error is precisely what we might expect from those who start with a low view of Scripture, as theological liberals do.

But lately even some traditionally conservative, professedly "Bible-believing" Christians have attacked the doctrine of Christ's literal, bodily return. A view fast gaining notoriety is *hyper-preterism* (sometimes called *full preterism* or "realized eschatology" by its advocates).[1] Hyper-preterists build their whole theology on a misunderstanding of Christ's words in Matthew 24:34: "Assuredly, I say to you, this generation will by no means pass away till all these things take place." They insist this means that every last detail of Bible prophecy had to have been completed before the death of those people living at the time He spoke, and actually *was* fulfilled in A.D. 70, during the turmoil and political upheaval that ensued when Jerusalem was sacked by Rome and most of its inhabitants were slaughtered.

In other words, according to hyper-preterists, Christ's Second Advent, the resurrection of the dead, and the Great White Throne judgment are all past events—so that absolutely no prophecy of Scripture remains unfulfilled. There is no future hope of Christ's return at all, they say. Hyper-preterists even claim that the universe in which we now live *is* the "new heavens and new earth" promised in passages like 2 Peter 3:13 and Revelation 21. That means this earth on which we now live is permanent. Sin and evil will never be finally eradicated from God's creation. Satan has already experienced as much defeat as he will ever experience. There is no tangible reality or physical existence beyond the grave. At death the believer simply becomes an eternally disembodied spirit, passing into the presence of God on a purely spiritual plane, with no hope of any future bodily resurrection. The souls of the wicked are similarly cast out of God's presence in a disembodied state.

So what do hyper-preterists do with the multitude of statements in Scripture that seem to contradict their view? For example, what of the promise of 1 Thessalonians 4:16-17? "The Lord Himself will descend from heaven with a shout, with the voice of an archangel, and with the trumpet of God. And the dead in Christ will rise first. Then we who are alive and remain shall be caught up together with them in the clouds to meet the Lord in the air. And thus we shall always be with the Lord." What of 1 Corinthians 15:22-24? "In Christ all shall be made alive. But each one in his own order: Christ the firstfruits, afterward those who are Christ's at His coming. Then comes the end, when He delivers the kingdom to God the Father, when He puts an end to all rule and all authority and power." What of verses 53-54? "This corruptible must put on incorruption, and this mortal must put on immortality. So when this corruptible has put on incorruption, and this mortal has put on immortality, then shall be brought to pass the saying that is written: 'Death is swallowed up in victory.'" And what of the dire judgment described in 2 Peter 3:10? "The day of the Lord will come as a thief in the night, in which the heavens will pass away with a great noise, and the elements will melt with fervent heat."

Taking a page from the liberals' handbook, hyper-preterists allegorize the meaning of those and all other prophetic passages, claiming they describe spiritual, not literal, realities. In other words, for the sake of interpreting Matthew 23:36 with an unwarranted wooden literalism, they will sacrifice the plain sense of every other prophecy about the return of Christ and end-times events.

This approach to Scripture ultimately has disastrous consequences for almost every fundamental doctrine of Christianity. For example, it obviously destroys the hope of any future resurrection of the dead. Hyper-preterists claim the complete fulfillment of the resurrection of the dead described in Revelation 20:4-15 and 1 Corinthians 15:51-52 already took place around A.D. 70. According to them, it was a spiritual, not a bodily, resurrection—and it is the only resurrection that will ever occur. Hyper-preterists have thus given up any hope of a literal, bodily resurrection of the saints.[2]

What of Christ's Second Coming? That too was a spiritual event that occurred in the church's first generation, they say; and there is no reason to expect a future literal fulfillment. Thus renouncing not only the plain meaning of Scripture but also every creed and doctrinal standard ever affirmed by any significant church council, denomination, or theologian in the entire history of the church, they deny that Christ will ever return to earth in bodily form.

The position sounds so bizarre that some may wonder if it seriously deserves to be refuted. How could anyone claim to believe the

Bible while denying that Christ will return bodily to earth? But the position has garnered an outspoken and influential following, especially among young believers with more zeal than knowledge. Judging from the high visibility and increasing numbers of people touting these views on the Internet and in other forums,[3] it appears they are having phenomenal success proselytizing other undiscerning souls to their view.

The bodily return of Christ is not a point on which the Scriptures are ambiguous or unclear. As the disciples watched the resurrected Christ ascend into heaven, Scripture tells us, "Two men stood by them in white apparel, who also said, 'Men of Galilee, why do you stand gazing up into heaven? This same Jesus, who was taken up from you into heaven, *will so come in like manner* as you saw Him go into heaven'" (Acts 1:10-11, emphasis added). He ascended in a visible, bodily form; he will return from heaven "in like manner." Nothing could be more plain.

Hyper-preterists have a ready response to that argument though: they deny that Christ ever truly ascended into heaven in bodily form.[4] They *must* take this position in order to preserve the "like manner" parallel between Christ's ascension and His return to earth.

Carrying the same poisonous hypothesis still one step further, some extreme hyper-preterists even deny that Christ was raised bodily from the dead. After all, 1 Corinthians 15:20-23 suggests that Christ was the "firstfruits" of all who will rise from the dead. His resurrection is therefore the pattern and prototype for everyone else who is to be raised from the dead. But having already swallowed the notion that believers are raised in a spiritual sense only, many hyper-preterists seem to have no qualms about also concluding that Christ Himself rose only in a spiritual sense from the grave. And thus they deny even the bodily resurrection of Christ. This destroys the very heart of all Christian doctrine. "For if the dead do not rise, then Christ is not risen. And if Christ is not risen, your faith is futile; you are still in your sins!" (1 Cor. 15:16-17). The apostle Paul seemed to have a theology very much like modern hyper-preterism in mind when he penned that verse.

Since they already deny so many cardinal doctrines of Christianity, it is no wonder that hyper-preterists are often seen slipping even further into unorthodox ideas. To give one example, Ward Fenley (arguably hyper-preterism's most influential author) claims that Christ actually *became* a sinner on the cross:

> He was not made sin while He lived His life. Yet upon the cross He became every terrible and unholy thing we ever committed. . . . My contention is that in Christ's immeasurable love for His children, He actually became everything we were in such a real way that He would go so far as to even pray to the Father, "Thou knowest My foolishness; and My sins are not hid from Thee."[5]

The hyper-preterist error is exactly like that of Hymenaeus and Philetus, who "strayed concerning the truth, saying that the resurrection is already past . . . they overthrow the faith of some" (2 Tim. 2:18). The apostle Paul was not reluctant to speak plainly about the seriousness of such soul-destroying error. Nor should we be hesitant to point out the dangers posed by such a serious departure from biblical truth. It is, after all, *heresy* of the worst stripe to deny the bodily return of Christ, and this particular brand of that heresy is currently overthrowing the faith of many.

THE FOLLY OF SENSATIONALIZING THE SECOND COMING

I believe the *fact* of the Second Coming is a cardinal doctrine. However, I must hasten to add that many of the *details* of biblical prophecy are surrounded with mystery, and it is a serious mistake to speak with dogmatic certainty about matters that are really nothing more than sheer conjecture. Jesus Himself said, "Of that day and hour no one knows, not even the angels in heaven, nor the Son, but only the Father. Take heed, watch and pray; for you do not know when the time is" (Mark 13:32-33). How could anything be *more* mysterious?

Yet at the opposite end of the spectrum from the hyper-preterists are people who seem to want to sensationalize everything
Scripture says about future events. They typically do this by
imposing modern headlines as an interpretive grid on the
Scriptures. This has been an increasingly popular, but completely
disastrous, approach to Bible prophecy for more than a hundred
years. I have in my library several books from various authors dat-
ing back to the beginning of the twentieth century, all of them
indulging in speculation about how certain people and current
events supposedly fulfill this or that prophecy. One book published around 1917 suggested that the events leading up to World
War I could only portend the Apocalypse. That book suggested the
generation living then would undoubtedly be the generation to be
caught away in the Rapture.

Twenty-five years later another group of authors observed the
rise of Hitler and suggested that the Führer perfectly fit the biblical
description of the Antichrist. Some of those books predicted the
Rapture would occur shortly, after which Hitler would gain world
domination and the Tribulation would begin. Others claimed the
Antichrist was Benito Mussolini or Josef Stalin. They all turned out
to be wrong.

After World War II many books were published claiming that
the founding of modern Israel had already triggered the countdown
to Armageddon, which could not be more than forty years away.
Those predictions were all made with great fanfare and solemn
gravity. And there was a proliferation of such books right through
the mid-1980s. All of them proved wrong.

And now, as we enter a new millennium, there is more such
speculation than ever. Religious television networks abound with
mock newscasts where self-styled experts in Bible prophecy continue to explain each week's headlines as if every major news event
were a direct fulfillment of some specific Bible prophecy. Christian
bookstores are filled with speculative books on Bible prophecy,
including the latest fad—novels that fuse current events with
prophecies drawn from Scripture in a fictional format. All of this

further encourages people to interpret Scripture in light of modern headlines instead of vice versa.

Worse, despite Jesus' plain statement, "you do not know when the time is," there is no shortage of speculation about dates (and even some dogmatic date-setters) in the evangelical world. In his 1970 mega-bestseller *The Late Great Planet Earth,* Hal Lindsey broadly hinted that he believed Christ would return by 1988:

> The most important sign in Matthew has to be the restoration of the Jews to the land in the rebirth of Israel. Even the figure of speech "fig tree" has been a historic symbol of national Israel. When the Jewish people, after nearly 2,000 years of exile, under relentless persecution, became a nation again on 14 May 1948 the "fig tree" put forth its first leaves.
>
> Jesus said that this would indicate that He was "at the door," ready to return. Then he said, "Truly I say to you, *this generation* will not pass away until all these things take place" (Matthew 24:34 NASB).
>
> What generation? Obviously, in context, the generation that would see the signs—chief among them the rebirth of Israel. A generation in the Bible is something like forty years. If this is a correct deduction, then within forty years or so of 1948, all these things could take place. Many scholars who have studied Bible prophecy all their lives believe that this is so.[6]

Lindsey's 1970 language sounds restrained compared to the more confident pronouncements he made as the forty-year target approached. In his 1980 book *The 1980s: Countdown to Armageddon,* Lindsey wrote, "The prophets told us that the rebirth of Israel—no other event—would be the sign that the countdown has begun. Since that rebirth, the rest of the prophecies have begun to be fulfilled quite rapidly. For this reason I am convinced that we are now in the unique time so clearly and precisely forecast by the Hebrew prophets."[7] Lindsey further stated that he believed the Rapture and the start of the Tribulation would occur in the 1980s.[8]

The forty-year time frame starting in 1948 was seized by others who transformed it into even more explicit dogma. As 1988 began, Edgar Whisenant published a book that quickly became a runaway best seller, *88 Reasons Why the Rapture Will Be in 1988*. Whisenant boldly assured readers that he had unlocked the mystery of the prophetic timetable, and the Rapture would occur during September 11-13, 1988, during Rosh Hashanah, the Jewish New Year, also known as *Yom Teru'ah* or the Day of the Blowing of the Shofar (described in Numbers 29:1).[9] Undaunted when his deadline passed, Whisenant changed the date of his prediction to 1989 and wrote a new book, *89 Reasons Why the Rapture Will Be in 1989*. But having discredited himself with the earlier false prediction, he had difficulty whipping up much excitement about the subsequent prediction (which, of course, turned out to be wrong too).

The date-setters were not finished, however. A few years later Harold Camping, president and general manager of the Family Radio network, published a book titled *1994*, in which he predicted the Lord's return on September 7, 1994.[10] Camping based his prediction on numerology, the founding of modern Israel, and other signs of the times. On his radio broadcasts he repeatedly claimed to be "more than 99 percent certain" his prediction was accurate. It wasn't.

There have been numerous lesser-known date-setters in recent years, and of course every one of them has been wrong. Every time this happens, it undermines the credibility of the Gospel in the minds of unbelievers who have heard such predictions and confuse them with the true Christian message. So many failed predictions also diminish Christians' confidence in their teachers. And, I fear, it subverts many people's expectancy that the Lord *could* return at any time. There is little doubt that the rise of hyper-preterism reflects a reaction to the shameless hype and unfulfilled predictions of evangelical end-times "experts" after so many decades of misguided predictions.

It doesn't help that the same self-styled experts change with the times, adjusting their interpretations of specific prophecies to match quickly-moving events. About thirty years ago Bible prophecy gurus were declaring confidently that the Soviet Union's rise to super-power status was loaded with biblical significance. Many believed that the Bible contained hints suggesting Russia would attack Jerusalem, and this conflict would usher in Armageddon. And when the 1980s turned out *not* to be the countdown to Armageddon but instead brought about the demise of communism, the fall of the Iron Curtain, and the breakup of the Soviet empire, the same self-proclaimed authorities on Bible prophecy simply adjusted their predictions accordingly and began to claim that even the fall of communism was clearly foretold in Scripture.

Current events are no guideline for interpreting Scripture. Those who continually adjust their understanding of Scripture to accommodate the latest headlines are treating Scripture like a wax figure that can be shaped in any form that suits their purposes. This is not how to handle the Word of God with integrity.

Furthermore, our preparedness for Christ's return should not be affected one way or the other by world events. As we shall see throughout our study in this book, Christ taught that we should be expectant and ready for Him to return at *any* time; and he also taught us to be prepared and stay faithful even if He tarries longer than we suppose. So true readiness for Christ's return involves *both* expectancy and patient endurance. Unfortunately, all the hype and sensationalism that characterizes most modern teaching about Bible prophecy actually undermines both sides of the balance.

THE MYSTERY OF THE SECOND COMING

Perhaps it is worth emphasizing again that *eschatology, the branch of theology that deals with future things,* is more enveloped in mystery than any other theological discipline. This is true by God's own design. Remember that even Christ, while on earth, said neither He Himself nor the angels in heaven knew the timing of the Second Coming: "Of that day and hour no one knows, not even the angels in heaven, nor the Son, but only the Father. Take heed, watch and pray; for you do not know when the time is" (Mark 13:32-33).

How could Christ, still fully God even while He was incarnated in human flesh, *not know* something as important as the timing of His own return? This certainly cannot mean He literally gave up His omniscience, for if He had actually divested Himself of any of the divine attributes, He would in effect have given up being God (Mal. 3:6; Heb. 13:8). Besides, Christ's omniscience is affirmed in many important instances in the Gospel accounts (e.g., John 16:30; 18:4; 21:17). But Scripture teaches that He was nonetheless truly human in every sense as well (Heb. 2:14-18). It appears that He was able to refrain from calling His omniscient knowledge to His conscious human mind when it was the Father's will for Him to do so (John 5:30); yet He did so without ever actually divesting Himself of omniscience or any other aspect of His deity. For example, He never gave up His omnipotence either (cf. John 10:18). Yet while on earth, because it suited the Father's plan, Christ willfully restrained the operation of His boundless divine power, so that His human body was subject to the normal limitations of human flesh (John 4:6). He voluntary subjected the use of *all* His divine attributes to the perfect will of the Father (John 5:19; 8:28). Surely this truth alone is a supreme, impenetrable mystery!

But no subject in all of Scripture is ever said to be *more* mysterious than the timing of Christ's return. No one but the Father knows the time; not Jesus during His earthly ministry, not the angels in heaven, not anyone else on earth—and particularly not those who make the boldest claims about knowing the secret details of God's prophetic agenda!

Since *Christ Himself* said He did not know the timetable of His return, isn't this a matter on which it behooves us all to show the utmost humility?

It is also instructive to remember that even prophets writing under divine inspiration were often left with mystery concerning the precise meaning of what they wrote—especially when it came to the who, what, and where of prophecies about future things. The apostle Peter wrote, "Of this salvation the prophets have inquired and searched carefully, who prophesied of the grace that would come to you, searching what, or what manner of time, the Spirit of Christ who was in them was indicating when He testified before-hand the sufferings of Christ and the glories that would follow" (1 Pet. 1:10-11). They did not understand, for example, how the prophecies of suffering and glory could be reconciled. Many of these things were mysterious to *everyone*, until Christ Himself explained them privately to the disciples after His resurrection (Luke 24:25-27).

That's why it is fitting that at the very beginning of this study we should acknowledge the depth of the remaining mystery surrounding the details of Christ's return. While the *fact* of the Second Coming is certainly a cardinal doctrine of Christianity, many of the *specifics* regarding how and when it will occur are, by the testimony of Scripture itself, set in the midst of incomprehensible mystery. And we must never lose sight of that. Detailed prophetic schemes and speculative eschatalogical timetables should never be treated as incontrovertible or fundamental dogma, nor made a principal test of orthodoxy and fellowship.

Unfortunately, this happens all the time. I know people who want to make eschatology the primary litmus test of all theology. Many of them are novices in the faith. They would not be prepared to give a coherent account of the doctrine of justification by faith. They may be ill-equipped to defend any of the fundamental doctrines of Christianity. But they consider themselves experts on the timing of the Rapture or the meaning of the seven seals in Revelation 5—7. Or they are convinced that there will be no Rapture or literal earthly kingdom at all, and they regard anyone who doesn't see things their way as an adversary. Such people, it seems, are constantly spoiling for a debate on eschatalogical fine points.[11]

Others who fall into this trap are by no means novices. They may be Christian leaders or theology professors, but they become imbalanced in their passion for a particular eschatological perspective, and they allow their zeal for these doctrines to become a barrier to fellowship with brethren who may disagree.

I know a man who insists that eschatology should be the starting point for the Christian worldview, and everything else we believe should be subject to our understanding of God's prophetic timetable. I can't imagine a more backward approach to either eschatology or the formulation of a Christian worldview. Our worldview ought to begin with the most vital and incontrovertible doctrines of Christianity—the matters on which Scripture speaks with the most clarity and the least amount of mystery. Eschatology is critically important insofar as it tells us the end of God's redemptive work and the culmination of His saving purpose. Certainly the hope of Christ's return is essential to the Christian worldview. But the speculative details of someone's eschatalogical timetable are not the proper focus or starting point. And there is no reason to isolate eschatology above the other theological categories as if prophetic details about the future were the most important features.

My advice to budding systematic theologians is this: master the fundamental issues of *soteriology, hamartiology, pneumatology, Christology, bibliology, theology proper*, and other essential points of Christian doctrine before settling into such a dogmatic stance on the eschatological fine points.

It's fine to have strong opinions on these matters. As far as Scripture allows, my own eschatalogical convictions are firm and definite, as you will note throughout this book. But given the mystery that surrounds so much of the prophetic revelation about the future, these are not matters on which we should be quarrelsome and quickly contentious. Our detailed prophetic diagrams should not be made tests of orthodoxy or grounds for separation from other believers. Aside from the aspects of Bible prophecy that are essential to the Christian message—such as the *fact* of Christ's bodily return, the resurrection of the dead, and the final triumph of Christ over all His enemies—these are not issues that should divide us from other Christians with whom we disagree.

Too many people are pugnacious about their views on the mysteries of biblical eschatology. Detailed prophetic calendars, dispensational charts, and debates about the order and arrangement of all the prophetic events simply do not warrant the amount of attention, the intensity of debate, or the level of intramural rancor they often generate between Christian brethren.

Worse, far too many Christians actually *do* break fellowship with other Christians who differ with them on speculative and secondary eschatological issues. But our humility as we approach such mysterious matters ought to be accompanied by charity for others whose perspectives are different.

Remember, despite the wealth of detailed prophecies in the Old Testament concerning Jesus' first advent, only a few people recognized the event when it occurred. Among these were the Magi—astrologers and occult practitioners who probably had little understanding of the Old Testament and very likely thought of Jehovah as a foreign deity. They were led to Christ by a star (Matt. 2:1-12). There were the shepherds to whom Christ's birth was announced by angels (Luke 2:8-18). There was also Simeon, a devout Israelite who had received a private revelation assuring him he would not die until he had seen the Messiah (vv. 25-35). And there was Anna, a godly widow who recognized the infant Christ—possibly also by a special revelation, for Scripture refers to her as "a prophetess" (vv. 36-38).

In other words, despite the many Old Testament prophecies about the Messiah's coming—the fact that He would be born in Bethlehem (Mic. 5:2), the fact that He would be virgin-born (Isa. 7:14), the fact that He would be preceded by a prophetic forerunner coming in the spirit and power of Elijah (Mal. 4:5-6; Isa. 40:3-4)—apparently *no one* relying on Old Testament prophecies alone recognized Him at His birth. History records that there was a high level of Messianic expectation in Israel around the time of Christ's coming, but when He arrived, He met no one's expectations.

It could very well be that every one of the modern "experts" in Bible prophecy will turn out to be wrong about the timing and the details of His Second Coming as well. Christ Himself seemed to suggest this when He said, "Therefore you also be ready, for the Son of Man is coming at an hour you do not expect" (Matt. 24:44; cf. Luke 12:40).

BE READY!

Clearly, then, much mystery clouds our full understanding of many of the features of our Lord's return. But if you think that is an excuse for ignorance, skepticism, or apathy on the whole subject of the Second Coming, think again. Repeatedly in Scripture we are urged to discern the signs of the times, to be watchful, and to be ready. Underscoring the mystery of His return for the disciples, Christ reminded them many times, "The Son of Man is coming at an hour you do not expect." But the corollary He inevitably stressed was: "Therefore you also be ready" (Luke 12:40). He rebuked people for being oblivious to the signs of the times: "Hypocrites! You know how to discern the face of the sky, but you cannot discern the signs of the times" (Matt. 16:3). The apostle John began the record of His apocalyptic visions with this promise: "Blessed is he who reads and those who hear the words of this prophecy, and keep those things which are written in it; for the time is near" (Rev. 1:3).

So these are issues we must study and gain a keen awareness of while we seek to deepen our understanding. We cannot afford to shelve eschatology just because it presents us with inscrutable features or back away from it just because it is such fertile ground for disagreement. We're commanded to know the signs of the times, to remain watchful, and to be ready whether Christ returns immediately or waits another thousand years. Scripture does give the diligent student plenty to be certain about.

Scripture is full of prophetic promises; so you cannot study Scripture without finding yourself neck-deep in eschatology. Faithful students—realizing that *all* Scripture is profitable for doctrine, reproof, correction, and instruction in righteousness—will study the prophetic portions of Scripture with the same diligence and enthusiasm they give the rest of God's Word.

I believe the prophetic passages of Scripture should be handled like any other portion of God's Word. The plain meaning of a text is the preferred interpretation. There's no reason to spiritualize or devise allegorical interpretations of Scripture if the literal sense makes good sense. Only if the context of a passage gives some compelling reason to assume the language is symbolic should we look for figurative meaning. Where the plain sense of Scripture makes good sense, there is no reason to seek any other sense.

For that reason, I believe *premillennialism* best reflects the correct understanding of Scripture. Premillennialism is the view that Christ will return to earth to judge the world and establish His kingdom here for 1,000 years, during which Satan will be bound.[12] Revelation 20 alone seems to settle this question definitively, and I know of no other passage of Scripture that would suggest any different scenario. On the contrary, all the Old Testament prophecies about the kingdom harmonize best with premillennialism.

Nonetheless, there are two other popular approaches to biblical eschatology. One is *amillennialism*, an interpretation that regards the reign of Christ described in Revelation 20 as an invisible, spiritual reality of indeterminate duration rather than a literal thousand-year earthly kingdom. Amillennialists believe the kingdom exists in a spiritual sense right now, and the next event on the prophetic calendar will be the return of Christ, followed immediately by the final judgment.

The other common approach to biblical eschatology is *postmillennialism*. This view suggests that the church will establish the earthly kingdom of Christ through preaching (and, according to some, through political means). Unlike amillennialists, postmillennialists believe in a literal earthly kingdom, but most believe Christ will reign over that kingdom from heaven, after which He will return to earth and institute final judgment.

Many commentators and theologians whom I respect hold to amillennialism or postmillennialism. Having studied carefully the arguments for all views, however, I am convinced premillennialism alone has solid *exegetical* support. Amillennialists and postmillennialists tend to hold their views because of theological, rather than textual, considerations. Both views require extraordinary handling of the prophetic passages of Scripture, demanding that the interpreter allegorize or spiritualize the meaning of such texts, rather than employing the same historical and grammatical principles of interpretation we apply to the rest of Scripture. But if we simply interpret the prophetic passages by the same hermeneutical method we use for the rest of God's Word, premillennialism emerges naturally from the text. A simple reading of Revelation 20 will reveal this; its plain, ordinary meaning is simply a succinct statement of premillennialism.

This book is therefore not so much an argument for premillennialism as it is a straightforward exegesis of some key biblical texts— *interpretation* most notably Christ's longest and most important eschatalogical *—doctrine* message, the Olivet Discourse. My hope is that as you are exposed *to final things such as death,* to the Word of God on these matters, it will stir in your heart a sincere expectation and earnest longing for Christ's return. And may that, in turn, spur you to an even deeper study of your own.

One

WHY CHRIST
MUST RETURN

Scripture predicted a time when skeptics would mock the very notion of Christ's return: "Scoffers will come in the last days, walking according to their own lusts, and saying, 'Where is the promise of His coming?'" (2 Pet. 3:3-4). There is no shortage of voices raising that chorus today.

For example, one group of self-styled authorities on Scripture claims to have discovered (using the techniques of modern literary criticism) that Christ did not even actually say the great majority of things attributed to Him by the New Testament. The so-called Jesus Seminar, a group of 200 liberal Bible scholars, convened to try to reach a consensus about which sayings of Christ are "authentic." This was deemed necessary because these particular scholars had already concluded that most of the words attributed to Christ in Scripture are spurious additions to the Gospel accounts. Their collective final decisions about which sayings are authentic were made by majority vote. The Seminar's verdict was no surprise to anyone familiar with liberal theology's approach to Scripture. These "scholars" concluded that of the more than 700 sayings attributed to Jesus in the Gospels, only thirty-one are unquestionably authentic—and more than half of those are actually duplicate statements from parallel passages. So all told, according to the Jesus Seminar scholars, only about fifteen of the New Testament sayings attributed to Jesus represent words He actually said.

In addition to the few statements they accepted as authentic, the scholars of the Jesus Seminar listed several more sayings they regarded as questionable but possibly authentic. They flatly rejected more than 80 percent of the words of Christ in Scripture—including, of course, all the major passages in which Christ promised His Second Coming.

"Where is the promise of his coming?" According to the Jesus Seminar scholars, Jesus made no such promise in the first place.

That kind of hard-core skepticism under a scholarly veneer is being mass-marketed widely these days. And the doctrine of the Second Coming is a particular target. One author writes:

> Jesus says: "Verily I say unto you, This generation shall not pass, till all these things be fulfilled."
>
> How could Jesus have been wrong about his return? A group of bible scholars known as the "Jesus Seminar" have studied the sayings of Jesus using the most recently discovered copies of ancient biblical manuscripts, other historical writings directly related to the times of Jesus and the early Christian church, scientific writing-style analysis, and other tools. After years of intense study and debate this group has come to the general consensus that over 80% of the words attributed to Jesus in the New Testament were not his words at all, but the interpretations and additions of early believers.
>
> It is very important to remember that nothing Jesus said was written down for at least an entire generation after his death. Stories of his words and ministry were circulated solely by word of mouth. This historical fact of the Oral Period is not disputed by any reputable bible scholar. . . . As difficult as it may be for bible-believers to accept, objective scholarly analysis has shown that the words of Jesus have been highly corrupted by the beliefs and words of early Christian believers.[1]

In the first place, that author misrepresents and grossly overstates the significance of the Jesus Seminar's work. The Seminar's findings have absolutely no "scientific" authority. They are merely the pooling of liberal opinion—little more than sheer conjecture grounded in sinful unbelief and skepticism. And it is misleading in the extreme to suggest that the liberal conclusions of the Jesus Seminar are "not disputed by any reputable bible scholar." The statement itself betrays the circular reasoning and closed-mindedness that is so typical of liberal "scholarship"; any scholar who disputes their theories is *automatically* regarded as not "reputable."

Nonetheless, multitudes have bought such lies—and chiefly, it seems, many clergymen. A few years ago I read about a survey given to a group of Protestant pastors at a church convention in Evanston, Illinois. Ninety percent said they have no expectation whatsoever that Christ will ever really return to earth.

The result of all this skepticism from so many scholars and clergy is that a whole segment of society regards the hope of the Second Coming as unenlightened nonsense and mindless fundamentalist fantasy. The arrogance of the scoffers has practically gained the status of conventional wisdom.

But Scripture is neither vague nor equivocal on the promise of Christ's return. A large proportion (by some accounts, as much as one-fifth) of Scripture is prophetic, and perhaps a third or more of the prophetic passages refer to the Second Coming of Christ or events related to it. It is a major theme of both Old Testament and New Testament prophecy.

And regardless of what the scoffers say, Jesus is coming. World history is barreling toward a conclusion, and the conclusion has already been ordained by God and foretold in Scripture. It could be soon, or it could be another thousand years (or more) away. Either way, God is not slack concerning His promise. Christ *will* return!

One ironic thing is that we live in a time when even the scoffers are in a state of rather fearful expectation. The frightening potential of worldwide destruction exists on several levels. Even the most impassioned secularists must acknowledge the very real potential that the world as we know it could end at any time—through nuclear war, a nuclear accident, an energy crisis, various ecological disasters, new killer viruses like AIDS (or worse), or even a cosmic collision of some kind. In fact, most people recognize that this world *cannot* exist forever. And we face constant reminders of this. For nearly the whole of the twentieth century, an unremitting string of books, articles, scientific studies, and even Hollywood productions have assaulted the public consciousness, warning us that if we do not collectively change the way we're living, we're going to go out of existence along with our little planet. In fact, the most vocal doomsayers today are not people who expect the return of Christ, but secularists who have recognized that this world and all life on it inevitably *will* end someday. They are right. It will end, but not because of ecological irresponsibility or human destructiveness.

How will it end? Can we know? Yes, we can. The Bible gives a very clear, direct answer. The world as we know it will end with the return of Jesus Christ. The history of the world will climax in His literal, bodily return to the earth.

This is as certain as any truth in Scripture. Here are nine reasons from Scripture by which we know that Christ is coming again:

THE PROMISE OF GOD DEMANDS IT

The Old Testament was full of Messianic promise. In fact, it's fair to say that the coming Messiah was the main focus of the Old Testament. The first hint of a Messianic Redeemer came in Genesis 3, right after Adam's fall, when God promised that the Seed of the woman would crush the serpent's head (v. 15). In the closing chapter of the final book of the Old Testament, God promised that "The Sun of Righteousness shall arise with healing in His wings" (Mal. 4:2). And between those two promises, the entire Old Testament is filled with prophecies of the coming Deliverer—at least 333 distinct promises, by one count.

More than a hundred of those prophecies were literally fulfilled at the first advent of Christ. Here are some key ones:

* Isaiah prophesied that he would be born of a virgin (Isa. 7:14; Matt. 1:18, 22-25).

• Micah foresaw that Bethlehem would be His birthplace (Mic. 5:2; Matt. 2:1).

• The experience of Old Testament Israel graphically foreshadowed His being called out of Egypt (Hos. 11:1;[2] Matt. 2:13-15).

• Isaiah foretold that He would be a descendant of Jesse (King David's father) and that He would be uniquely anointed with the Spirit of God (Isa. 11:1-5; Matt. 3:16-17).

• Zechariah prophesied that He would enter Jerusalem riding on a colt, the foal of a donkey (Zech. 9:9; Luke 19:35-37).

• Psalm 41:9 predicted that He would be betrayed by a familiar friend with whom he had shared a meal (cf. Matt. 10:4).

• Zechariah prophesied that He would be stricken and His sheep scattered, anticipating that He would be forsaken by His own closest disciples (Zech. 13:7; Mark 14:50).

• Zechariah also foretold the exact price of Judas' betrayal (thirty pieces of silver), as well as what would become of the betrayal money (Zech. 11:12-13; Matt. 26:15; 27:6-7).

• Isaiah foretold many details of the crucifixion (Isa. 52:14-53:12; Matt. 26:67; 27:29-30, 57-60).

• David foretold many additional details of the tortures Christ endured at the cross, including His last cry to the Father, the piercing of His hands and feet, and the parting of his garments (Ps. 22; Matt. 27:35, 42-43, 46; John 19:23-24).

• David also prophetically foretold that none of Christ's bones would be broken (Ps. 34:20; John 19:33).

• And elsewhere David alluded to the Resurrection (Ps. 16:10; cf. Acts 2:27; 13:35-37).

All the prophecies dealing with the first advent of Christ were fulfilled precisely, literally. His riding on a donkey, the parting of his garments, the piercing of His hands and feet, and the vivid prophecies of His rejection by men in Isaiah 53—all these *might* have been interpreted symbolically by Old Testament scholars before Christ. But the New Testament record repeatedly reports that such things were fulfilled in the most literal sense, so "that the Scriptures of the prophets might be fulfilled" (Matt. 26:56; cf. 2:15; 4:14-16; 8:17; 12:17-21; 13:35; 21:4-5; 27:35; John 12:38; 15:25; 19:24, 28).

In some cases Old Testament prophecies about Christ were ful-filled with a literalism that could not have been anticipated by even the most careful Old Testament scholars. For example, Psalm 69 seems to be a lament from David while he was under attack from his enemies and in deep distress. Nothing in the Psalm itself gives us a clue that any prophecies are contained in it. In fact, in verse 5 David refers to his own foolishness and sins. So these words came from the heart of David to describe his own anguish at being hated without a cause. Yet there is a deeper, prophetic meaning. Typologically, David prefigured the Redeemer. And the New Testament indicates that certain phrases in this psalm refer to Christ in an even greater way than they referred to David. "Zeal for Your house has eaten me up" (v. 9) is shown to be a prophecy that was lit-erally fulfilled by Christ in Mark 11:15-17 (compare John 2:14-17). Verse 21, "They also gave me gall for my food, and for my thirst they gave me vinegar to drink," turns out to be a prophecy that was lit-erally fulfilled on the cross (Matt. 27:34).

It stands to reason, then, that the remaining two-thirds of Old Testament Messianic prophecies will also be fulfilled literally. And that requires the return of Jesus Christ to this earth.

When Christ took up the scroll in His hometown synagogue at Nazareth and began to read, in God's perfect timing the scheduled reading for that week came from Isaiah 61. Luke 4:17-21 records the incident:

And He was handed the book of the prophet Isaiah. And when He had opened the book, He found the place where it was written: "The Spirit of the LORD is upon Me, because He has anointed Me to preach the gospel to the poor; He has sent Me to heal the broken-hearted, to proclaim liberty to the captives and recovery of sight to the blind, to set at liberty those who are oppressed; to proclaim the accept-able year of the LORD." Then He closed the book, and gave it back to the attendant and sat down. And the eyes of all who were in the synagogue were fixed on Him. And He began to say to them, "Today this Scripture is fulfilled in your hearing."

If we compare the text with Isaiah 61, we see that Christ stopped reading abruptly in the middle of a sentence. Here's the full text of Isaiah 61:1-3:

The Spirit of the LORD God is upon Me, because the LORD has anointed Me to preach good tidings to the poor; He has sent Me to heal the brokenhearted, to proclaim liberty to the captives, and the opening of the prison to those who are bound; to proclaim the accept-able year of the LORD, and the day of vengeance of our God; to comfort all who mourn, to console those who mourn in Zion, to give them beauty for ashes, the oil of joy for mourning, the garment of praise for the spirit of heaviness; that they may be called trees of righteousness, the planting of the LORD, that He may be glorified. (emphasis added)

The rest of the chapter from Isaiah goes on to describe the bless-ings of the millennial kingdom, when "the earth brings forth its bud, as the garden causes the things that are sown in it to spring forth. So the LORD God will cause righteousness and praise to spring forth before all the nations" (v. 11).

Christ deliberately stopped reading mid-sentence because "the day of vengeance of our God" pertains to His second advent, not His first. Many Old Testament prophecies seemed to telescope Messianic events this same way, so that it was not always immedi-ately obvious when one portion of a prophecy referred to the first coming of Christ, while another portion referred to His second coming. Employing the Old Testament alone, it would have been very difficult to discern any distinction between the two classes of Messianic prophecies.

But here are some familiar Old Testament prophecies about Christ that await fulfillment at His Second Coming:

Psalm 2. We know this speaks of Christ. Verse 7 is quoted several times in the New Testament and is applied to Him: "You are My Son, today I have begotten You" (cf. Acts 13:33; Heb. 1:5; 5:5). Yet many aspects of this psalm await future fulfillment. Verse 6 suggests an earthly reign that is yet to be realized: "Yet I have set My King on My holy hill of Zion." The kingdom and the judgment described in verses 8-9 also have yet to be fulfilled literally: "I will give You the nations for Your inheritance, and the ends of the earth for Your possession. You shall break them with a rod of iron; You shall dash them to pieces like a potter's vessel."

Isaiah 9:6-7. This familiar passage also seems to have both the first and second comings of Christ in view: "For unto us a Child is born, unto us a Son is given. . . ." That plainly refers to His first advent, anticipating the angel's promise to Mary in Luke 1:35. But the rest of Isaiah 9:6-7 describes Him as a king in glory on David's throne:

> *And the government will be upon His shoulder. And His name will be called Wonderful, Counselor, Mighty God, Everlasting Father, Prince of Peace. Of the increase of His government and peace there will be no end, upon the throne of David and over His kingdom, to order it and establish it with judgment and justice from that time forward, even forever.*

Christ Himself pointed to His second coming as the time when He would assume that throne in a literal sense: "When the Son of Man comes in His glory, and all the holy angels with Him, *then* He will sit on the throne of His glory" (Matt. 25:31, emphasis added).

Micah 4:3. This passage echoes the promise of a kingdom of peace under His rule: "He shall judge between many peoples, and rebuke strong nations afar off; they shall beat their swords into plowshares, and their spears into pruning hooks; nation shall not lift up sword against nation, neither shall they learn war anymore." Again the literal fulfillment of that prophecy awaits a second advent of the Savior.

Jeremiah 23:5. Here the Word of God expressly states that the future kingdom of Christ is to be an earthly one: "'Behold, the days are coming,' says the LORD, 'that I will raise to David a Branch of righteousness; a King shall reign and prosper, and execute judgment and righteousness *in the earth*'" (emphasis added). He must return to establish that kingdom on earth.

Zechariah 14:4-9. Zechariah describes the Second Coming graphically:

> *And in that day His feet will stand on the Mount of Olives, which faces Jerusalem on the east. And the Mount of Olives shall be split in two, from east to west, making a very large valley; half of the mountain shall move toward the north and half of it toward the south. Then you shall flee through My mountain valley, for the mountain valley shall reach to Azal. Yes, you shall flee as you fled from the earthquake in the days of Uzziah king of Judah. Thus the LORD my God will come, and all the saints with You.*

> *It shall come to pass in that day that there will be no light; the lights will diminish. It shall be one day which is known to the LORD— neither day nor night. But at evening time it shall happen that it will be light.*

> *And in that day it shall be that living waters shall flow from Jerusalem, half of them toward the eastern sea and half of them toward the western sea; in both summer and winter it shall occur. And the LORD shall be King over all the earth. In that day it shall be—"The Lord is one," and His name one.*

That describes the glorious appearing of Christ, which is yet to come, when He returns to set all things right. Nothing like that occurred at His first coming. Like much that pertains to Messianic prophecy in the Old Testament, it awaits future fulfillment at the Second Coming of Christ.

Scripture says God "cannot lie" and that He will not change His mind (Titus 1:2; Num. 23:19). What He has promised, He will do. And much of what He promised about Christ requires that the

Savior return to earth in triumph in order to bring it to pass. The truthfulness of the Bible is at stake.

THE TEACHING OF CHRIST DEMANDS IT

Christ's own words also make it clear that He will return. His earthly teaching was filled with references to His Second Coming. Many of His parables spoke of it. In fact, the Gospels include entire chapters dealing with events related to the Second Coming (Matt. 24—25; Luke 21).

On the night of His betrayal Christ told the disciples, "I go to prepare a place for you. And if I go and prepare a place for you, I will come again and receive you to Myself" (John 14:2-3). Not only is the credibility of God at stake in the Second Coming, but so is the credibility of His Son. *If Jesus doesn't return He's a liar.*

But His own words are a divine guarantee that He *will* be back. "Indeed, let God be true but every man a liar" (Rom. 3:4).

Christ, on trial for His life, defended His own deity with a bold declaration of the Second Coming in the most triumphant terms. He told the High Priest, "You will see the Son of Man sitting at the right hand of the Power, and coming with the clouds of heaven" (Mark 14:62).

And a short time before that, as Christ had unfolded the panorama of future events to His disciples on the Mount of Olives, He told them, "As the lightning comes from the east and flashes to the west, so also will the coming of the Son of Man be" (Matt. 24:27). He added this vivid description:

> *"The sign of the Son of Man will appear in heaven, and then all the tribes of the earth will mourn, and they will see the Son of Man coming on the clouds of heaven with power and great glory. And He will send His angels with a great sound of a trumpet, and they will gather together His elect from the four winds, from one end of heaven to the other."*
>
> —VV. 30-31

Several of the parables Christ told to illustrate His kingdom emphasized the truth of the Second Coming. He did this "because [the disciples] thought the kingdom of God would appear immediately" (Luke 19:11). So He stressed repeatedly that the aspect of His kingdom in operation since His first coming until now is spiritual and invisible (Luke 17:20-21), whereas the visible, earthly aspect of His kingdom pertained to His Second Coming. So His parables often pictured a ruler who, having gone to a far-off country, returns to rule in person. The parable in Luke 19:12-27 expressly pictures "a certain nobleman [who] went into a far country to receive for himself a kingdom and to return" (v. 12). And upon returning, "having received the kingdom" (v. 15), he executes judgment and distributes joint rulership in his kingdom to his servants who were faithful in his absence (vv. 15-19).

Similarly, three parables in the Olivet Discourse—the parable of the two servants (Matt. 24:45-51), the parable of the ten virgins (Matt. 25:1-13), and the parable of the talents (Matt. 25:14-30)—all underscore the certainty of Christ's return.

Nor is that all. In the book of Revelation, Christ repeatedly said, "Surely I am coming quickly" (Rev. 22:20; cf. 2:5, 16; 3:11; 22:7, 12). The Revelation unfolds "the things which will take place after this" (1:19; 4:1). And the crown and culmination of it all is Christ's triumphant return, described in chapter 19.

So Christ has repeatedly assured us of His return. He made these promises during His earthly ministry, just before His ascent to heaven, and even in a vision to John from His throne in heaven. He wanted both friends and enemies to know that He would be back. His very credibility depends on the Second Coming.

THE TESTIMONY OF THE HOLY SPIRIT DEMANDS IT

Since "God . . . cannot lie" (Titus 1:2), His promise guarantees Christ's return. Jesus is truth incarnate (John 14:6); so His teaching also infallibly confirms the fact of the Second Coming. The Holy

Spirit, who is called "the Spirit of truth" (John 14:17; 15:26), also testifies of the Second Coming of Christ.

The apostle Paul wrote these words under the Holy Spirit's inspiration in Corinthians 1:4-7: "I thank my God always concerning you for the grace of God which was given to you by Christ Jesus, that you were enriched in everything by Him in all utterance and all knowledge, even as the testimony of Christ was confirmed in you, so that you come short in no gift, eagerly waiting for the revelation of our Lord Jesus Christ."

It was the Holy Spirit who confirmed the testimony of Christ in them, and it was the Holy Spirit who gave them their expectancy for Christ's coming. Moreover, the Holy Spirit as the divine author of Scripture thereby confirms the promise of Christ's coming (2 Pet. 1:20-21).

Elsewhere Paul wrote, "Our citizenship is in heaven, from which we also eagerly wait for the Savior, the Lord Jesus Christ" (Phil. 3:20). He encouraged the Colossians by saying, "When Christ who is our life appears, then you also will appear with Him in glory" (Col. 3:4). And he had much to say about the Lord's return in his epistles to the Thessalonians. Here's a sample:

> *For the Lord Himself will descend from heaven with a shout, with the voice of an archangel, and with the trumpet of God. And the dead in Christ will rise first. Then we who are alive and remain shall be caught up together with them in the clouds to meet the Lord in the air. And thus we shall always be with the Lord.*
>
> —1 THESS. 4:16-17

The Holy Spirit further confirmed the promise of Christ's return through the writer of Hebrews: ". . . so Christ was offered once to bear the sins of many. To those who eagerly wait for Him He will appear a second time" (9:28).

You'll find that promise reiterated in the epistle of James: "Therefore be patient, brethren, until the coming of the Lord. See how the farmer waits for the precious fruit of the earth, waiting patiently for it until it receives the early and latter rain. You also be patient. Establish your hearts, for the coming of the Lord is at hand" (5:7-8).

Peter penned similar Spirit-inspired promises. Here's one: "Gird up the loins of your mind, be sober, and rest your hope fully upon the grace that is to be brought to you at the revelation of Jesus Christ" (1 Pet. 1:13). And another: "When the Chief Shepherd appears, you will receive the crown of glory that does not fade away" (5:4).

The Spirit also confirmed this truth through the apostle John. First John 3:2 is one of the most blessed promises in Scripture: "Beloved, now we are children of God; and it has not yet been revealed what we shall be, but we know that when He is revealed, we shall be like Him, for we shall see Him as He is."

Again and again the Holy Spirit testifies through the writers of the New Testament that Christ is coming a second time. His testimony, through the pens of the men whom He employed as instruments to write the inspired Word of God, adds a third infallible witness to that of the Father and the Son. Through the inerrant Scriptures, the Holy Spirit is still testifying that Jesus is coming.

THE PROGRAM FOR THE CHURCH DEMANDS IT

God's plan for the church also demands the return of Christ. He is currently "visit[ing] the Gentiles to take out of them a people for His name" (Acts 15:14). He is gathering His elect into one great body, the church. And the church's role is to be like a pure bride for God's own Son, ready to be presented to Him at His Second Coming.

And that is precisely the imagery the apostle Paul uses in 2 Corinthians 11:2: "I am jealous for you with godly jealousy. For I have betrothed you to one husband, that I may present you as a chaste virgin to Christ."

Scripture repeatedly portrays Christ at His Second Coming as a Bridegroom coming to claim his bride. The apostle John's vision of heaven included a vivid description of the wedding supper:

> *And I heard, as it were, the voice of a great multitude, as the sound of many waters and as the sound of mighty thunderings, saying, "Alleluia! For the Lord God Omnipotent reigns! Let us be glad and rejoice and give Him glory, for the marriage of the Lamb has come, and His wife has made herself ready." And to her it was granted to be arrayed in fine linen, clean and bright, for the fine linen is the righteous acts of the saints. Then he said to me, "Write: 'Blessed are those who are called to the marriage supper of the Lamb!'" And he said to me, "These are the true sayings of God."*
>
> —REV. 19:6-9

That symbolism is based on the pattern that was in vogue for Oriental weddings during New Testament times. In fact, that pattern was based on ancient traditions that reached far back into Old Testament history. Every marriage had three vital elements, each symbolized in the relationship of Christ with His church.

The bridal price. In New Testament times, marriages were arranged by parents. Parents would get together and agree by contract to have their children marry one another—sometimes before the bride and bridegroom had even met. These marriage contracts were binding, and to seal the contract, the husband-to-be or his father had to pay a bridal price or dowry.[3] This ensured the bride's financial security. The money, though paid to the bride's father, was meant to be kept for her in case her husband died or deserted her (cf. Gen. 31:15). The bridal price also included gifts for the bride (cf. Gen. 24:53; Judg. 1:15). Once the dowry was paid, the union contract was recognized by law and could only be terminated by divorce—even before any wedding vows were exchanged and the physical union was consummated (cf. Matt. 1:18-19).

The New Testament employs this imagery to describe the relationship between Christ and the church. When He died on the cross, the price He paid with His own blood was like a legal payment for His marriage to His church—the dowry. Paul repeatedly referred to the church as a purchased possession of the heavenly Bridegroom. This symbolism was so vital that Paul even employed it to teach what a godly marriage should be like. He instructed husbands, "Love your wives, just as Christ also loved the church and gave Himself for her, that He might sanctify and cleanse her with the washing of water by the word, that He might present her to Himself a glorious church, not having spot or wrinkle or any such thing, but that she should be holy and without blemish" (Eph. 5:25-27). Paul's farewell speech to the Ephesian elders included this charge: "Shepherd the church of God which He purchased with His own blood" (Acts 20:28). That was, by the way, the most costly dowry ever paid. And although the marriage has not yet been consummated, it is legally in effect and will be binding forever. That is the very thing that guarantees our security. Nothing can separate us from the love of Christ.

The betrothal. The betrothal in an ancient marriage was officially marked by a ceremony in which the bride and the bridegroom met in the presence of witnesses and gave gifts to each other. This ceremony would have looked very similar to a modern wedding ceremony except that it took place long before the marriage could be consummated—sometimes a year or more in advance. Then the bride and her husband-to-be would each return to their respective homes. During the period between the betrothal and the consummation of the marriage, the man was occupied with preparing a place for his bride. This usually meant building an addition or an attachment to his father's house, so that the new couple would have a secure place to begin their lives together. Joseph and Mary had entered such a betrothal before Gabriel brought her the heavenly message about the miracle of virgin conception and birth (Luke 1:26-38; Matt. 1:18-25).

Again this beautifully pictures Christ and His church. He has given her gifts (Eph. 4:8), and He has gone to prepare her a place in His Father's house (John 14:2). This entire age between His first and Second Coming is therefore like the betrothal period. The church is espoused to Christ. The bridal price has been paid; gifts have been given. The union is forever binding. But it awaits a final consummation.

The marriage feast. The final phase of a marriage occurred when the bridegroom and his friends would go to the bride's house for a marriage ceremony and a great feast. This event is depicted in the story of the marriage at Cana (John 2:1-11) and the parable of the virgins in Matthew 25:1-13.

Likewise, the marriage supper of the Lamb and His bride will signal the consummation of God's plan for the church. That feast cannot occur until Christ returns for His bride (Rev. 19:6-16). And that is precisely God's plan for the church. Therefore Christ *must* return.

The institution of marriage itself is a beautiful metaphor that pictures Christ's love for His church. And if He were not going to return to claim her, it would spoil the whole point. So God's program for the church demands the return of Jesus Christ.

THE CORRUPTION IN THE WORLD DEMANDS IT

Here's another reason Christ must return: to judge the world. Matthew 16:27 records Jesus' words, "The Son of Man will come in the glory of His Father with His angels, and then He will reward each according to his works." Scripture portrays the return of Christ as the "blessed hope" of the church (Titus 2:13). But for the world of unbelievers, the return of Christ is a terrifying prospect, because His coming means immediate judgment on them. In John 5:25-29 He promised this coming judgment:

> "Most assuredly, I say to you, the hour is coming, and now is, when the dead will hear the voice of the Son of God; and those who hear will live. For as the Father has life in Himself, so He has granted the Son to have life in Himself, and has given Him authority to execute judgment also, because He is the Son of Man. Do not marvel at this; for the hour is coming in which all who are in the graves will hear

*His voice and come forth—those who have done good, to the resur-
rection of life, and those who have done evil, to the resurrection of
condemnation."*

Scripture repeatedly associates Christ's return with final, com-
prehensive judgment. Jude 14-15 says, "Behold, the Lord comes
with ten thousands of His saints, to execute judgment on all, to convict all who are ungodly among them of all their ungodly deeds
which they have committed in an ungodly way, and of all the harsh
things which ungodly sinners have spoken against Him."
Paul told the Thessalonian believers:

*The Lord Jesus [will be] revealed from heaven with His mighty
angels, in flaming fire taking vengeance on those who do not know
God, and on those who do not obey the gospel of our Lord Jesus
Christ. These shall be punished with everlasting destruction from the
presence of the Lord and from the glory of His power, when He
comes, in that Day, to be glorified in His saints and to be admired
among all those who believe, because our testimony among you was
believed.*

—2 THESS. 1:7-10

Scripture tells us that all judgment has been committed to
Christ (John 5:22). And Scripture repeatedly portrays Him returning to earth in order to carry out that judgment. The consummate
picture of this is Revelation 19:11-16:

*Now I saw heaven opened, and behold, a white horse. And He who
sat on him was called Faithful and True, and in righteousness He
judges and makes war. His eyes were like a flame of fire, and on His
head were many crowns. He had a name written that no one knew
except Himself. He was clothed with a robe dipped in blood, and His
name is called The Word of God. And the armies in heaven, clothed
in fine linen, white and clean, followed Him on white horses. Now
out of His mouth goes a sharp sword, that with it He should strike
the nations. And He Himself will rule them with a rod of iron. He*

Himself treads the winepress of the fierceness and wrath of Almighty
God. And He has on His robe and on His thigh a name written:
KING OF KINGS AND LORD OF LORDS.

Jesus *must* return in order to execute just retribution on sinners
and carry out the judgment He has promised.

THE FUTURE OF ISRAEL DEMANDS IT

So it is clear that God's dealings with the church and the world both
necessitate the return of Christ. Did you realize His plan for Israel
also demands the Second Coming?

Zechariah 12:10 includes this promise: "I will pour on the
house of David and on the inhabitants of Jerusalem the Spirit of
grace and supplication; then they will look on Me whom they
pierced. Yes, they will mourn for Him as one mourns for his only
son, and grieve for Him as one grieves for a firstborn." That salvation of Israel has not yet happened, but it will. "In that day a fountain shall be opened for the house of David and for the inhabitants
of Jerusalem, for sin and for uncleanness" (13:1). The whole of
Zechariah 14 goes on to detail that great day of salvation for Israel,
which will occur at the Lord's return.

Romans 11:25-27 says this: "Blindness in part has happened to
Israel until the fullness of the Gentiles has come in. And so all Israel
will be saved, as it is written: 'The Deliverer will come out of Zion,
and He will turn away ungodliness from Jacob; for this is My
covenant with them, when I take away their sins.'"

Paul was clearly describing a future reality. He was looking forward to a time when "all Israel will be saved." He pictured the people of God as an olive tree. Israel, the natural branches of the
domestic tree, failed to produce fruit; so God broke the branches off
and grafted in branches from a wild olive tree, representing the elect
Gentiles. Apparently in Paul's day Gentiles were already being
added to the church in greater numbers than Jewish converts. And
Paul reminded the Gentile converts, "You, being a wild olive tree,

were grafted in among them, and with them became a partaker of the root and fatness of the olive tree" (v. 17). But a time is coming when the natural branches will be grafted back into the olive tree (vv. 23-24). And Paul expressly connects that phenomenon with the return of Christ, the Deliverer who will come out of Zion (v. 26).

THE VINDICATION OF CHRIST DEMANDS IT

Here's another important reason Christ must return: It is inconceivable that the last public view the world would have of Jesus Christ would be that of a bleeding, dying, crucified criminal, covered with blood, spit, and flies, hanging naked in a Jerusalem twilight. Did you realize that after His resurrection, He never appeared in a public venue before unbelievers? Plenty of *believers* saw Him, touched Him, spoke to Him, and gave unanimous testimony that He was risen from the dead. But there is no record that unbelievers ever saw Him. If they did, they no doubt became believers immediately. Believers who saw Him certainly had all their doubts dispelled, as illustrated in Thomas's encounter with the risen Christ (John 20:24-29).

In 1 Corinthians 15:5-8 Paul lists those who witnessed the risen Lord: "He was seen by Cephas, then by the twelve. After that He was seen by over five hundred brethren at once, of whom the greater part remain to the present, but some have fallen asleep. After that He was seen by James, then by all the apostles. Then last of all He was seen by me also, as by one born out of due time." Notice that there is not an unbeliever in that list.

So the last time the world saw him on display, He was humiliated, suffering, and hanging on the cross. His glory has not yet been displayed to the world.

But the world *will* see it. Scripture says, "Christ was offered once to bear the sins of many. To those who eagerly wait for Him He will appear a second time" (Heb. 9:28). "He is coming with clouds, and every eye will see Him, even they who pierced Him. And all the tribes of the earth will mourn because of Him" (Rev.

1:7). "As the lightning comes from the east and flashes to the west, so also will the coming of the Son of Man be" (Matt. 24:27).

A couple of important passages of Scripture set prophecies about His humiliation and His subsequent public exaltation side by side, suggesting that one cannot occur without the other. Psalm 22:16–18 prophesied in detail the treatment He would receive at the hands of those who put Him to death: "Dogs have surrounded Me; the congregation of the wicked has enclosed Me. They pierced My hands and My feet; I can count all My bones. They look and stare at Me. They divide My garments among them, and for My clothing they cast lots." But the climax of that same psalm anticipates the glory that will be on display when He returns to earth: "All the ends of the world shall remember and turn to the LORD, and all the families of the nations shall worship before You. For the kingdom is the LORD's, and He rules over the nations" (vv. 27–28).

Matthew 26 also sets his first-advent suffering and His Second-Coming glory alongside one another. Matthew 26:67–68 describes the treatment Christ received at the hands of those who arrested Him: "They spat in His face and beat Him; and others struck Him with the palms of their hands, saying, 'Prophesy to us, Christ! Who is the one who struck You?'" They mocked Him. Played games with Him. Plucked His beard. Humiliated Him. And ultimately they executed Him. Is that how Jesus is to be remembered in the eyes of the world? Is that His last public appearance on earth?

In this very context, Jesus Himself indicated that it would not be. "The high priest . . . said to Him, 'I put You under oath by the living God: Tell us if You are the Christ, the Son of God!' Jesus said to him, 'It is as you said. Nevertheless, I say to you, hereafter you will see the Son of Man sitting at the right hand of the Power, and coming on the clouds of heaven'" (vv. 63–64). Thus the promise of future exaltation was expressed graphically by Jesus Himself, in the midst of His own humiliation.

The indignity and shame of the crucifixion took place in full view of a scoffing crowd. How public will the display of His glory be? "Every eye will see him" (Rev. 1:7). "There will be signs in the sun, in the moon, and in the stars; and on the earth distress of nations, with perplexity, the sea and the waves roaring; men's hearts failing them from fear and the expectation of those things which are coming on the earth, for the powers of the heavens will be shaken. Then they will see the Son of Man coming in a cloud with power and great glory" (Luke 21:25-27). The Savior who was humiliated and taunted and put to death in a public display of humanity's hatred of God will return as conquering Lord in view of the entire world. He *must* return.

THE DESTRUCTION OF SATAN DEMANDS IT

There is still another vital reason Christ must return—to vanquish the devil. Satan, though an already-defeated foe as far as Christians are concerned, still exercises a kind of dominion over this world. Three times in the Gospel of John Christ referred to the devil as "the ruler of this world" (12:31; 14:30; 16:11). In 2 Corinthians 4:4 the apostle Paul calls Satan "the god of this age." In Ephesians 2:2 he calls him "the prince of the power of the air, the spirit who now works in the sons of disobedience." And in Ephesians 6:12 he refers to Satan's hierarchy of evil spirits as "principalities . . . powers . . . the rulers of the darkness of this age . . . spiritual hosts of wickedness in the heavenly places." First John 5:19 says, "The whole world lies under the sway of the wicked one."

There's a sense in which Satan still runs the world. How did he gain this power? At creation God gave dominion over all creation to Adam. But when Adam succumbed to Satan's enticements, obeying the devil rather than God, Adam in effect abdicated his place of dominion and left that authority to the devil. Satan has been the ruler of this world ever since. He has no legal right to rule. He's a usurper. Yet God allows him to remain in power.

When Christ atoned for sin, He dealt Satan the crushing blow, redeeming Adam's fallen race and destroying Satan's claim to world dominion. "Therefore God also has highly exalted Him and given Him the name which is above every name, that at the name of Jesus every knee should bow, of those in heaven, and of those on earth, and of those under the earth, and that every tongue should confess that Jesus Christ is Lord, to the glory of God the Father" (Phil. 2:9-11). Christ is the only rightful ruler of this world, and when He returns He will overthrow and destroy Satan completely.

Revelation 5 pictures this drama in graphic terms. The apostle John describes his vision of heaven; God was seated on His throne, holding a scroll that had seven seals. The scroll also had writing on the inside and back (v. 1).

That is a description of this world's title deed. In biblical times, as is true even today, title deeds were vital records that proved who owned a piece of property. In the Old Testament era, land could not permanently change ownership. Tracts of land could be used temporarily as collateral for a loan or be given away for a period of time in payment of a debt. But land could not be sold permanently (cf. Lev. 25:23). During the Jubilee year (which occurred every fifty years) all land that had changed hands was to be returned to the family of its rightful owner (v. 10). Even between Jubilee years, those wishing to recover their family's lands could redeem their property for a fair price. Jeremiah redeemed some of his family's land by such means (Jer. 32:6-7), and he describes how the transaction was carefully recorded in a title deed:

> *I signed the deed and sealed it, took witnesses, and weighed the money on the scales. So I took the purchase deed, both that which was sealed according to the law and custom, and that which was open; and I gave the purchase deed to Baruch the son of Neriah, son of Mahseiah, in the presence of Hanamel my uncle's son, and in the presence of the witnesses who signed the purchase deed, before all the Jews who sat in the court of the prison.*
>
> —VV. 10-12

Those signatures would have been recorded with seals. A typical title deed would have multiple seals, just like the scroll in Revelation 5. And the typical first-century reader of John's vision would have understood this scroll as a legal document, a title deed. It is, I believe, the very title deed to this earth.

No one could lawfully open a title deed except the rightful heir designated by the deed itself. That is why there was writing on the outside of the scroll. The writing on the outside was a summary of what was in the document, identifying who had the right to open it. Jewish deeds were, by law, witnessed by at least three signatures, with three seals—and sometimes more, depending on the importance of the document.

The seven-sealed scroll in Revelation 5 is clearly a document of monumental importance, and the fact that God Himself was holding the scroll while angels were loudly seeking someone worthy to open it (vv. 2-3) suggests that whoever was qualified to open the scroll must be someone very worthy indeed.

The situation seemed such a dilemma to John that he started crying: "I wept much, because no one was found worthy to open and read the scroll, or to look at it" (v. 4). But there was no question in heaven about who had authority to open that title deed. "One of the elders said to me, 'Do not weep. Behold, the Lion of the tribe of Judah, the Root of David, has prevailed to open the scroll and to loose its seven seals'" (v. 5). Christ as Son of God was the legitimate Heir to all creation (Ps. 2:6-8; Heb. 1:1-2). And He also earned the right to the title deed of the earth because He redeemed the world from the dominion of Satan.

Having already paid the redemption-price, Christ *must* return to earth to establish His dominion here. Revelation 6—7 describes the opening of the seven seals, each one resulting in a unique judgment. The final seal brings utter silence in heaven, followed by seven trumpet blasts. And again each of the seven blasts unleashes a new wave of judgment (chapters 8—11). Following the trumpets, seven vials representing seven final judgment-plagues are poured out on the earth (chapter 16). Finally, after one last-ditch effort by Satan to retain his unlawful dominion over the earth, Christ Himself returns. Revelation 19 describes the scene, when He comes suddenly and destroys His enemies. In chapter 20 Satan is chained and thrown into a bottomless pit and then finally confined forever to an eternal lake of fire. With that, Christ's final victory over Satan is complete.

Scripture consistently portrays Christ's return to earth as the necessary prelude to Satan's ultimate doom. Therefore Christ *must* return to earth to accomplish the final destruction of His archenemy.

THE HOPE OF THE SAINTS DEMANDS IT

And here's a final reason the Lord must return to earth: Only His glorious, triumphant return can fulfill the hope of the saints. God is not in the business of giving false hope. He knows what we are waiting for. He knows the longing of our hearts. His Word gives us every reason to long for the appearing of our Lord Jesus Christ— and He will not disappoint that blessed hope.

Peter saw the promise of Christ's return as a great comfort for the people of God in their times of trial—"that the genuineness of your faith, being much more precious than gold that perishes, though it is tested by fire, may be found to praise, honor, and glory at the revelation of Jesus Christ" (1 Pet. 1:7).

Paul encouraged believers to have that same hope:

> *We ourselves boast of you among the churches of God for your patience and faith in all your persecutions and tribulations that you endure, which is manifest evidence of the righteous judgment of God, that you may be counted worthy of the kingdom of God, for which you also suffer; since it is a righteous thing with God to repay with tribulation those who trouble you, and to give you who are troubled rest with us when the Lord Jesus is revealed from heaven with His mighty angels.*
>
> —2 THESS. 1:4-7

All true believers long for the day when Jesus Christ will return to earth. Paul characterizes all Christians as those who "love his appearing" (2 Tim. 4:8, KJV). John adds, "Now we are children of God; and it has not yet been revealed what we shall be, but we know that when He is revealed, we shall be like Him, for we shall see Him as He is" (1 John 3:2). In other words, the return of Christ will instantly usher in the fullness of our glorification.

For all these reasons Christ *must* return. We are taught throughout the New Testament to look for His coming, to long for it, and to wait patiently and expectantly for it. This has been the blessed hope of every true child of God since the beginning of the age. And the fulfillment of that hope is now closer than it has ever been.

The apostle John added these words: "And everyone who has this hope in Him purifies himself, just as He is pure" (v. 3). This is the test of a healthy eschatology: Is your hope a sanctifying influence on your soul? Rather than getting caught up in hype and hysteria about current events and newspaper headlines, are you looking beyond the commotion of this world with the realization that you could soon meet Christ face to face, and are you preparing your heart and soul for that? Instead of despairing, as some do, over how long Christ has delayed His coming, are you filled with hope and expectation? Are you eager and watching, knowing that the time still draws nigh? That is the attitude to which Scripture calls us.

The Second Coming is not supposed to make us stop what we're doing to wait for the Lord's return. And neither should it motivate us to focus all our attention on the events and political developments of this world. Instead, it should direct our hearts toward Christ, whose coming we await—and it should prompt us to purify ourselves as He is pure.

Two

IS CHRIST'S COMING IMMINENT?

Christ could come at any moment. I believe that with all my heart—not because of what I read in the newspapers, but because of what I read in Scripture.

From the very earliest days of the church, the apostles and first-generation Christians nurtured an earnest expectation and fervent hope that Christ might suddenly return at any time to gather His church to heaven. James, writing what was probably the earliest of the New Testament epistles, expressly told his readers that the Lord's return was imminent:

> *Be patient, brethren, until the coming of the Lord. See how the farmer waits for the precious fruit of the earth, waiting patiently for it until it receives the early and latter rain. You also be patient. Establish your hearts, for* the coming of the Lord is at hand. *Do not grumble against one another, brethren, lest you be condemned.* Behold, the Judge is standing at the door!
> —5:7-9, EMPHASIS ADDED

Peter echoed that same expectation when he wrote, "The end of all things is at hand; therefore be serious and watchful in your prayers" (1 Pet. 4:7). The writer of Hebrews cited the imminent return of Christ as a reason to remain faithful: "Let us consider one another in order to stir up love and good works, not forsaking the assembling of ourselves together, as is the manner of some, but exhorting one another, and so much the more as you see the Day approaching" (Heb. 10:24-25). He wrote, "Yet a lit-tle while, and He who is coming will come and will not tarry" (v. 37). And the apostle John made the most confident pronounce-ment of all: "Little children, it is the last hour; and as you have heard that the Antichrist is coming, even now many antichrists have come, by which we know that it is the last hour" (1 John 2:18). When John recorded his vision in the book of Revelation, he prefaced it by saying that these things "must shortly take place" (1:1).

The New Testament writers often wrote of Christ's "appear-ing," and they never failed to convey the sense that this could hap-pen imminently. "And now, little children, abide in Him, that when He appears, we may have confidence and not be ashamed before Him at His coming" (1 John 2:28; cf. 3:2; Col. 3:4; 2 Tim. 4:8; 1 Pet. 5:4).

All those texts suggest that in the early church, expectation of Christ's imminent return ran high. A solid conviction that Christ could return at any time permeates the whole New Testament. When the apostle Paul described the Lord's coming for the church, he used personal pronouns that show he clearly was convinced he himself might be among those who would be caught up alive to meet the Lord: *"We* who are alive and remain until the coming of the Lord . . . *we* who are alive and remain shall be caught up together with them in the clouds to meet the Lord in the air" (1 Thess. 4:15, 17, emphasis added). He obviously looked for Christ to return in his lifetime. He furthermore made it plain that a watchful, hopeful expectancy about Christ's Second Coming is one of the godly atti-tudes divine grace teaches all believers: "For the grace of God that brings salvation has appeared to all men, teaching us that, denying ungodliness and worldly lusts, we should live soberly, righteously, and godly in the present age, *looking for the blessed hope and glorious appearing of our great God and Savior Jesus Christ*" (Titus 2:11-13, emphasis added).

Will the Tribulation Precede Christ's Coming for the Church?

Nonetheless, some students of Bible prophecy today insist Christians should not have any immediate expectation of Christ's return. Instead, they say, we should be looking for the beginning of the seven-year *Tribulation* period, the fulfillment of certain judgments and preliminary signs, the rise of the Antichrist, or all of the above. When they talk about future things, the emphasis is heavily weighted toward dread and disaster for the people of God. As far as they are concerned, "the blessed hope" becomes relevant only *after* the church has gone through the Tribulation.

At first glance, this position seems not altogether devoid of biblical support. After all (as we will see in the chapters to come), when Christ outlined the events of the last days, He included many prophecies about tribulation and hardship, and He said these signs would precede and point to His return (Matt. 24:21, 30).

The epistles also contain prophecies about apostasy and persecution in the last days preceding Christ's return. For example, the apostle Paul forewarned Timothy of perilous times that would come (2 Tim. 3:1-6). He told the younger pastor, "The Spirit expressly says that in latter times some will depart from the faith" (1 Tim. 4:1), and he went on to describe an apostasy that would precede and signify Christ's return to earth.

Those who believe the church must suffer through the hardships of the Tribulation period invariably cite 2 Thessalonians 2:1-3 as proof:

> *Concerning the coming of our Lord Jesus Christ and our gathering together to Him, we ask you, not to be soon shaken in mind or troubled, either by spirit or by word or by letter, as if from us, as though the day of Christ had come. Let no one deceive you by any means; for that Day will not come unless the falling away comes first, and the man of sin is revealed, the son of perdition.* (emphasis added)

So on the one hand, the New Testament is permeated with an eager sense of expectancy and conviction that the blessed hope of Christ's return is imminent. On the other hand, we are warned about trouble and affliction that will precede Christ's return. How can we reconcile these two threads of prophecy? How can we cultivate a daily expectation of Christ's return if these preliminary signs must yet be fulfilled before He returns?

Several points must be borne in mind. First, all the general "signs of the times" given in the New Testament *have* been fulfilled and *are being* fulfilled before our eyes. They are, in fact, characteristics of the entire church age. Apostasy and unbelief, self-love and sin, wars, rumors of wars, and natural disasters have all been common throughout the church age. Practically every generation of Christians since the time of Christ has believed they were seeing the end-times signs fulfilled before their very eyes. So how are *we* to know whether our own time is the true "last days" of Bible prophecy or just more of the same general apostasy and calamity that have characterized the entire Christian era?

The apostle John settled that question under the Holy Spirit's inspiration when he wrote, "Little children, it is the last hour; and as you have heard that the Antichrist is coming, even now many antichrists have come, by which we know that it is the last hour" (1 John 2:18). The church was *already* in the last days even before the apostolic era ended. In fact, "last days" is a biblical term for the Christian era itself (Heb. 1:1-2). This entire age is a prelude to the final culmination of human history. These *are* the last days—and so was the early church era.

Second, nothing in the New Testament ever suggests we should defer our expectation of Christ's appearing until other preliminary events occur. The one apparent exception is 2 Thessalonians 2:1-3 (quoted in full above), which says, "that Day [the Day of the Lord] will not come unless the falling away comes first, and the man of sin is revealed." That is obviously a key text for those who believe the Tribulation is next on the prophetic agenda and that the church should be expecting the reign of Antichrist rather than the return of

Christ. Indeed, if 2 Thessalonians 2:1-3 actually means Christ's coming for the church cannot occur until after seven years of Tribulation, it nullifies everything the New Testament teaches about the imminence of Christ's return.

But look carefully at the context of 2 Thessalonians 2. The Thessalonian Christians had been confused and upset by some false teachers (possibly people pretending to speak for the apostle) who were teaching that the persecutions and sufferings they were currently experiencing were the very judgments associated with *the Day of the Lord*. (That expression always refers to a time of apocalyptic judgment; cf. Isa. 13:9-11; Amos 5:18-20; 1 Thess. 5:2-3; 2 Pet. 3:10; Rev. 6:17; 16:14.) Many in the Thessalonian church, in the midst of their own severe hardship and distress, had evidently believed that lie, and they believed it meant they themselves had become objects of God's final apocalyptic wrath. Obviously they were deeply troubled by this, for in his earlier epistle Paul had encouraged them by telling them of *the Rapture* (1 Thess. 4:14-17)—the coming of Christ for His church. Paul had even instructed them to comfort one another with the promise of Christ's coming for them (v. 18).

But now, in a time of severe persecution and trial, the Christians at Thessalonica had fallen prey to the false idea that God was already pouring out His final wrath—and that *they* were among the objects of that wrath. They obviously feared they had missed the Rapture and were about to be swept away in the final and epochal judgments of the Day of the Lord.

So Paul wrote, "Now, brethren, concerning the coming of our Lord Jesus Christ and our gathering together to Him, we ask you, not to be soon shaken in mind or troubled, either by spirit or by word or by letter, as if from us, as though the day of Christ had come" (2 Thess. 2:1-2). "The coming of our Lord Jesus Christ and our gathering together to Him" is a clear reference to the *Rapture*. "The day of Christ" is *the Day of the Lord* (in fact, the older manuscripts use the expression "day of the Lord" in this verse).

There were two aspects of the error troubling the Thessalonian church. One was the notion that they had missed the Rapture. The other was the accompanying fear that they had already entered into the apocalyptic judgment that signaled that the day of the Lord had arrived already.

So when Paul says, *"that Day* will not come unless the falling away comes first, and the man of sin is revealed, the son of perdition" (2 Thess. 2:3, emphasis added), he is talking about the Day of the Lord and its apocalyptic judgment, not the Rapture. He was not suggesting that the coming of Christ for the church would be delayed until after the Tribulation events had all played out. He was certainly not suggesting that the Thessalonians should defer their hope of Christ's coming for them until the end of the Tribulation. He had spent his entire first epistle urging them to be watchful and expectant and to encourage one another with the news of Christ's imminent return (cf. 1 Thess. 1:10; 4:14-18; 5:6, 9, 11). If the apostle now meant to teach them that all the events of the Tribulation must be fulfilled *before* Christ could return for them, that would be scant "comfort" indeed. In fact, it would overturn everything the New Testament has to say about Christ's return being imminent, comforting, and hopeful.

So the consistent teaching of the New Testament is that Christians should be looking for the imminent coming of Christ for His church, and 2 Thessalonians 2:1-4 is no exception.

How Could Christ's Coming Have Been Imminent in the Early Church?

Some argue that Christ's coming could not possibly have been imminent for the early church, given the obvious fact that 2,000 years later He has still not returned. Skeptics often ridicule Christianity or challenge the inerrancy of Scripture on that very ground. After all, the verses cited at the beginning of this chapter do prove that James, Peter, John, Paul, and the writer of Hebrews all believed Christ's return was very near—"at the door" (James 5:9); "at hand" (Phil. 4:5; 1 Pet. 4:7); "approaching" (Heb. 10:25); "coming quickly" (Rev. 3:11; 22:7).

How can it be, then, that 2,000 years later Christ still has not returned? Could the apostles have been in error about the timing? That is precisely what some skeptics claim. Here's a typical excerpt from a newsletter whose sole aim is to attack the inerrancy of Scripture:

> Paul, himself, showed . . . that he was among those who awaited the imminent return of Christ. Yet, as the history of that era clearly shows, all was for nought. No messiah appeared. . . . The NT repeatedly says the messiah was to return in a very short time. Yet, mankind has waited for nearly 2,000 years and nothing has occurred. By no stretch of the imagination can that be considered "coming quickly." . . . It is, indeed, unfortunate that millions of people still cling to the forlorn hope that somehow a messiah will arise to extract them from their predicament. How many years (2,000, 10,000, 100,000) will it take for them to finally say, "We can only conclude that we are the victims of a cruel hoax"?[1]

What shall we make of this charge against the truthfulness of Scripture? Does the passing of 2,000 years indeed prove that Christ's coming was not imminent in the early church era and that the apostles were mistaken?

Certainly not. Remember the clear statement of Christ in Matthew 24:42: "You do not know what hour your Lord is coming." The exact time remains hidden from us, as it was from the apostles. But Christ could nonetheless come at any time. The Judge is still at the door. The day is still at hand. There are no other events that must occur on the prophetic calendar before Christ comes to meet us in the air. He could come at any moment. And it is in *that* sense that Christ's coming is imminent. In the very same sense, His coming was imminent even in the days of the early church.

I suppose it is *also* possible that Christ could delay His coming another 2,000 years or longer. Given the rapid decline of society, I do not see how that is possible, but neither did the apostles when they surveyed the state of the world in their time. He still *could* delay His coming. That is why Christ taught us to be prepared, whether He comes immediately or delays longer than we think possible (cf. Matt. 24:42—25:13).

In any case, the passing of 2,000 years is no reproach whatsoever against the faithfulness of God or the trustworthiness of His Word. This is precisely the point Peter made when he anticipated the scoffers who would arise, mocking the promise of Christ's return (2 Pet. 3:3-4). Peter's reply to those scoffers? "With the Lord one day is as a thousand years, and a thousand years as one day" (v. 8). The amount of earthly time that passes is of no consequence. It is certainly irrelevant from God's timeless point of view. A moment is like many aeons in His mind, and aeons pass like moments. He is not bound by time as we are, and no amount of time can ever nullify His faithfulness. "The Lord is not slack concerning His promise, as some count slackness, but is longsuffering toward us, not willing that any should perish but that all should come to repentance" (v. 9).

In other words, the real reason for the Lord's delay is not that He is negligent or careless in fulfilling His promises, but simply because He is longsuffering and kind, delaying Christ's coming and the wrath that will accompany it while He calls people unto salvation. And Christ will not return before the merciful purposes of God are complete. Far from suggesting apathy or neglect on God's part, the long delay before Christ's appearing simply underscores the remarkable depth of His nearly inexhaustible mercy and long-suffering.

And therefore the fact that 2,000 years have elapsed is utterly irrelevant to the doctrine of Christ's imminent return. Christ's coming is *still* imminent. It could occur at any moment. The command to be ready and watchful is as applicable to us as it was to the early church. In fact, the return of Christ should be an even *more* urgent issue for us because it is drawing nearer with the passing of each day. We still do not know *when* Christ is coming, but we do know that we are 2,000 years closer to that event than James was in those earliest days of the Christian era, when the Holy Spirit moved him to warn the church that the coming of the Lord was "at hand" and the Judge was already standing "at the door."

Why Is Christ's Imminent Return So Important?

Why is it so important to believe that Christ could come at any moment? Because, as we saw at the conclusion of the preceding chapter, the hope of Christ's imminent coming has a powerful sanctifying and purifying effect on us. "Everyone who has this hope in Him purifies himself, just as He is pure" (1 John 3:3). The knowledge that Christ's coming is drawing closer should motivate us to prepare, to pursue Christlikeness, and to put off all the things that pertain to our former lives without Christ.

The apostle Paul took this very line of argument near the end of his epistle to the Romans. He reminded the believers at Rome of our duty to love our neighbors as ourselves, saying love is the one principle that fulfills all God's moral commands (Rom. 13:8-10). Then, stressing the urgency of living in obedience to this great commandment, he wrote:

> *And do this, knowing the time, that now it is high time to awake out of sleep; for* now our salvation is nearer than when we first believed. *The night is far spent,* the day is at hand. *Therefore let us cast off the works of darkness, and let us put on the armor of light. Let us walk properly, as in the day, not in revelry and drunkenness, not in lewdness and lust, not in strife and envy. But put on the Lord Jesus Christ, and make no provision for the flesh, to fulfill its lusts.*
> —VV. 11-14

That is the apostle Paul's wake-up call to the church. Christ's return is approaching. The time now is nearer than when we first believed. Every moment that passes brings Christ's return even closer. How are we to redeem the time? He calls for a three-part response that perfectly sums up the Christian's proper perspective on the imminent possibility of Christ's return.

Wake Up! "Awake out of sleep," he pleads (v. 11), and he underscores both the urgency of this command and the imminency of Christ's return with four phrases: "now it is high time"; "our salvation is nearer" (v. 11); "The night is far spent"; and "the day is at hand" (v. 12). Time is short; opportunity is fleeting. The Lord is coming soon, and the event draws nearer every moment. The time to obey is now. The only time we can take for granted is now. And since there is no guarantee of more time, it is unconscionable to defer our obedience.

Consider this: the apostle Paul was stressing the urgency of this commandment in *his* day, 2,000 years ago. He believed the coming of Christ was near and getting nearer by the moment. How much *more* urgent are these things for our time? "Now our salvation is nearer" (v. 11)—2,000 years nearer, to be precise. Now is certainly not the time to let down our guard or fall asleep. Although some might be tempted to think the long delay means Christ's coming is no longer an urgent matter, a moment's thought will reveal that if we believe Christ was speaking the truth when He promised to come again quickly, we *must* believe that the time is drawing nearer by the moment. And the urgency is not lessened by the delay but heightened.

It is perfectly natural for infidels, skeptics, and unbelievers to think Christ's delay means He will not fulfill His promise (2 Pet. 3:4). But no genuine believer should ever think that way. Rather than despairing because He tarries, we ought to realize that the time is nearer now than it has ever been. He *is* coming. As we saw in the previous chapter, His Word guarantees that He will come. Our hope should be growing stronger, not diminishing, as He delays his coming.

When Paul writes, "And do this, knowing the time" (Romans 13:11), he employs a Greek word for "time" (*kairos*) that speaks of an age or an era, not the time (*chronos*) told by a clock. "Knowing the time" therefore speaks of understanding this age, being discerning, like "the sons of Issachar who had understanding of the times, to know what Israel ought to do" (1 Chron. 12:32). Christ rebuked the Pharisees for lacking this same kind of discernment. "When it is evening you say, 'It will be fair weather, for the sky is red'; and in the morning, 'It will be foul weather today, for the sky is red and threatening.' Hypocrites! You know how to discern the face of the sky, but you cannot discern the signs of the times [kairos]" (Matt. 16:1-3).

Perhaps Paul had seen signs of spiritual lethargy or dullness among the believers at Rome. No doubt life in that great city held many distractions and earthly enticements that drew hearts away from the earnest hope of Christ's appearing. Like the society in which we live, Roman life catered to the flesh, offering many material comforts and earthly amusements. Perhaps they were inclined to forget they were living in the last days. Spiritually, they were falling asleep.

It sometimes seems as if the entire church today is in an even worse state of spiritual drowsiness. There is widespread indifference concerning the Lord's return. Where is the sense of expectation that characterized the early church? The sad legacy history will record about the church of our generation is that as we neared the dawn of a new millennium, most Christians were far more concerned about the arrival of a computer glitch known as the "millennium bug" than they were with the arrival of the Millennial King!

Too many Christians in our time have settled into a state of insensate lethargy and inactivity—an unresponsiveness to the things of God. They are like Jonah, fast asleep in the hold of the ship while raging storms threaten to sweep us away (Jon. 1:5-6). They are like the foolish virgins who "while the bridegroom was delayed . . . all slumbered and slept" (Matt. 25:5). It is high time to awake from that slumber.

Paul sent a similar wake-up call to the church at Ephesus: "'Awake, you who sleep, arise from the dead, and Christ will give you light.' See then that you walk circumspectly, not as fools but as wise, redeeming the time, because the days are evil" (Eph. 5:14-16). Never was such an alarm more needed than today. In the words of our Lord Himself, "Watch therefore, for you do not know when the master of the house is coming—in the evening, at midnight, at the crowing of the rooster, or in the morning—lest, coming suddenly, he find you sleeping" (Mark 13:35-36).

When Paul says "our salvation is nearer than when we first believed" (Rom. 13:11), he is speaking, of course, about the *consummation* of our salvation. He was not suggesting that the Romans were unregenerate. He was not telling them their *justification* was a yet-future reality. He was reminding them that the culmination of what began at their regeneration was drawing closer by the moment. "Salvation" in this context refers to our *glorification*, the final goal of God's saving work (Rom. 8:30). Throughout Scripture this is connected with the appearing of Christ. "We know that when He is revealed, we shall be like Him" (1 John 3:2). We "eagerly wait for the Savior, the Lord Jesus Christ, who will transform our lowly body that it may be conformed to His glorious body" (Phil. 3:20-21). "When Christ who is our life appears, then you also will appear with Him in glory" (Col. 3:4). "He will appear a second time, apart from sin, for salvation" (Heb. 9:28). Notice that the writer of Hebrews employs the word *salvation* the same way Paul uses it in Romans 13:11.

This final aspect of salvation is what Paul referred to a few chapters earlier, in Romans 8:23: "We ourselves groan within ourselves, eagerly waiting for the adoption, the redemption of our body." That is the aspect of our salvation that is nearer than when we first believed, and it only awaits Christ's coming.

So Paul's penetrating appeal here in Romans 13 assumes that Christ's return is imminent. If another eschatalogical age (*kairos*)—especially the Tribulation—were going to occur prior to Christ's return for the church, Paul would have surely pointed to the onset of that era and urged the Romans to prepare for it. But far from warning them that a dark era of tribulation was in their future, what he told them was virtually the opposite: "The night is far spent, the day is at hand" (v. 12). The *kairos* of persecution, hardship, and darkness was "far spent" (*prokoptō* in the Greek text, meaning "advancing quickly" or "being driven out"). Daylight—the final consummation of our salvation when Christ returns to take us to glory—is imminent.

We have no idea how much sand remains in the hourglass of human history. But we ought to realize that a lot of sand has passed through the hourglass since the apostle Paul said the dawning of daylight was already at hand. How much more urgent is this wake-up call for the church today!

The nighttime of Satan's dominion will soon give way to the dawn of Christ's coming for His own. The apostle Paul used precisely the same imagery of darkness and dawn when he wrote to the Thessalonians:

> But concerning the times and the seasons, brethren, you have no need that I should write to you. For you yourselves know perfectly that the day of the Lord so comes as a thief in the night. For when they say, "Peace and safety!" then sudden destruction comes upon them, as labor pains upon a pregnant woman. And they shall not escape. But you, brethren, are not in darkness, so that this Day should overtake you as a thief. You are all sons of light and sons of the day. We are not of the night nor of darkness. Therefore let us not sleep, as others do, but let us watch and be sober. For those who sleep, sleep at night, and those who get drunk are drunk at night. But let us who are of the day be sober, putting on the breastplate of faith and love, and as a helmet the hope of salvation. For God did not appoint us to wrath, but to obtain salvation through our Lord Jesus Christ.
>
> —1 THESS. 5:1-9

God did not appoint us to wrath. The day of wrath that will come in the Tribulation is not what we are to be preparing for. The sudden appearing of Christ to take us to glory is our hope. Wake up. Be sober. Be alert. Your redemption draws nigh.

Throw Off! The approaching of dawn means it's time for a change of garments. "Let us cast off the works of darkness, and let us put on the armor of light" (Rom. 13:12). Paul's imagery evokes the picture of a soldier who has spent the night in a drunken orgy. Still clad in the garments of his sin, he has fallen into a drunken sleep. But dawn is approaching, and now it is time to wake up, throw off the clothes of night, and put on the armor of light.

The Greek verb translated "cast off" was a term that spoke of being ejected or expelled forcefully. The Greek term is used only three other times in the New Testament, and in each case it speaks of excommunication from a synagogue (John 9:22; 12:42; 16:2). So the term carries the idea of renouncing and forsaking sin (or the unrepentant sinner) with vigor and conviction. Paul is calling for an act of repentance. He wants them to cast off—excommunicate or break fellowship with—"the works of darkness." It is the same expression he uses in Ephesians 5:11: "Have no fellowship with the unfruitful works of darkness, but rather expose them."

Paul often employs the imagery of changing garments to describe the putting off of sin and the old man. "Put off, concerning your former conduct, the old man which grows corrupt according to the deceitful lusts" (Eph. 4:22). "Put off all these: anger, wrath, malice, blasphemy, filthy language out of your mouth. Do not lie to one another, since you have put off the old man with his deeds" (Col. 3:8-9). Notice the twofold putting off: "you *have put off* the old man with his deeds"; but *keep putting off* "all these" works of darkness. The picture this evokes is that of Lazarus—raised from the dead, given new life, but still bound in old grave-clothes that needed to be put off (cf. John 11:43-44).

Employing similar imagery, the writer of Hebrews urges believers to "lay aside every weight, and the sin which so easily ensnares us, and let us run with endurance the race that is set before us" (12:1). There he pictures the Christian like an athlete, stripped of all encumbrances and ready to run. There is much we must throw aside if we are to be prepared for the coming day. James sums it up succinctly: "lay aside all filthiness and overflow of wickedness" (Jas. 1:21). And Peter echoes the thought: "laying aside all malice, all deceit, hypocrisy, envy, and all evil speaking" (1 Pet. 2:1).

Put On! There's another aspect of being prepared for the Lord's appearing. We're not fully prepared for the dawn of the new day unless we have put on the appropriate attire: "put on the armor of light . . . put on the Lord Jesus Christ" (Rom. 13:12, 14).

Again the imagery is that of a soldier who had spent the night in drunken carousing. He had stumbled home and fallen asleep in clothes that were now wrinkled and befouled with the evidence of his reveling. Day was dawning. It was time to wake up, to cast off the old clothes, and to put on something clean and polished and battle-ready. "Armor" suggests warfare, and that is fitting. Though the return of Christ is imminent, that is no warrant to forsake the battle. There is never any suggestion in Scripture that His people should sit on a hillside somewhere to await His coming.

In fact, between now and His coming we are locked in a battle "against principalities, against powers, against the rulers of the darkness of this age, against spiritual hosts of wickedness in the heavenly places" (Eph. 6:12). The nearness of our Lord's return doesn't mitigate the seriousness of the battle. Now is not the time to slacken our diligence; in fact, the opposite is true. We should engage the battle with new vigor, knowing that the time is short. "Therefore take up the whole armor of God, that you may be able to withstand in the evil day, and having done all, to stand" (v. 13).

In other words, we're not off-duty soldiers, free to carouse and indulge in the fleshly pleasures of nightlife. We are on duty, and our Commander-in-Chief might appear at any moment. Therefore, "Let us walk properly, as in the day, not in revelry and drunkenness, not in lewdness and lust, not in strife and envy" (Rom. 13:13). The Christian who is not living a holy and obedient life with heavenly priorities is a Christian who does not grasp the significance of the Lord's imminent return. If we genuinely are expecting our Lord to appear at any time, that blessed hope should move us to be faithful and to walk properly, lest our Lord return to find us walking improperly, disobeying or dishonoring Him. In Christ's own words, "Watch therefore, for you do not know when the master of the house is coming—in the evening, at midnight, at the crowing of the rooster, or in the morning—lest, coming suddenly, he find you sleeping. And what I say to you, I say to all: Watch!" (Mark 13:35-37).

There's more: "But put on the Lord Jesus Christ, and make no provision for the flesh, to fulfill its lusts" (Rom. 13:14). Again, when we are glorified, we will be instantly conformed to the image of Christ—made as much like Him as it is possible for human beings to be. Christlikeness is therefore the goal toward which God is moving us (Rom. 8:29). Even now the process of sanctification should be conforming us to His image. As we grow in grace, we grow in Christlikeness. We are to become a reflection of Christ's character and His holiness. And that is what Paul means when he writes, "put on the Lord Jesus Christ." We are to pursue sanctification, to follow after Christ in our conduct and character, to let His mind be in us, and to let His example guide our walk (Phil. 2:5; 1 Pet. 2:21).

Paul compared his pastoral duty, discipling the Galatians, to birth pains as he sought to bring them to Christlikeness: "I labor in birth again until Christ is formed in you" (Gal. 4:19). Writing to the Corinthians he also described sanctification as the process by which they would be remade in Christ's likeness: "We all, with unveiled face, beholding as in a mirror the glory of the Lord, are being transformed into the same image from glory to glory, just as by the Spirit of the Lord" (2 Cor. 3:18). In other words, we progress from one level of glory to another as we progress toward the ultimate goal. So "put on the Lord Jesus Christ" is simply a command to pursue sanctification (the whole theme of Romans 12—16).

When Paul told the Galatians, "as many of you as were baptized into Christ have put on Christ" (Gal. 3:27), he was in essence saying that sanctification begins at conversion. From the first moment of faith, we are clothed in His righteousness. That is justification. In the words of the prophet Isaiah, "I will greatly rejoice in the LORD, my soul shall be joyful in my God; for He has clothed me with the garments of salvation, He has covered me with the robe of righteousness" (61:10).

But that is just the beginning of what it means to put on Christ. Justification is a once-for-all completed event, but sanctification is an ongoing process. And the command to "put on the Lord Jesus Christ" in Romans 13 is a command to pursue the Christlikeness of sanctification.

The hope of Christ's imminent return is therefore the hinge on which a proper understanding of sanctification turns.

Let's review some of the key texts that speak of the imminence of Christ's return, and notice specifically what kind of practical duties this doctrine places on us.

- *Steadfastness*: "Be patient. Establish your hearts, for the coming of the Lord is at hand" (Jas. 5:8).
- *Kindness*: "Do not grumble against one another, brethren, lest you be condemned. Behold, the Judge is standing at the door!" (Jas. 5:9).
- *Prayer*: "The end of all things is at hand; therefore be serious and watchful in your prayers" (1 Pet. 4:7).
- *Faithfulness in assembling together and encouraging one another*: "Let us consider one another in order to stir up love and good works, not forsaking the assembling of ourselves together, as is the manner of some, but exhorting one another, and so much the more as you see the Day approaching" (Heb. 10:24-25).
- *Holy conduct and godliness*: "Therefore, since all these things will be dissolved, what manner of persons ought you to be in holy conduct and godliness" (2 Pet. 3:11).
- *Purity and Christlikeness*: "When He is revealed, we shall be like Him, for we shall see Him as He is. And everyone who has this hope in Him purifies himself, just as He is pure" (1 John 3:2-3).

Those cover several broad categories, embracing every aspect of our sanctification. The hope of Christ's imminent return is a catalyst and an incentive for all these things—every fruit of the Spirit, every Christian virtue, everything that pertains to holiness and Christlikeness, everything that belongs to life and godliness.

That's why it's so important to cultivate a watchful expectancy for the imminent coming of Christ. The point is not to make us obsessed with earthly events. In fact, if your interest in the return of Christ becomes a consuming fixation with what is happening in this world, you have utterly missed the point. The knowledge that Christ's return is imminent should turn our hearts toward heaven, "from which we also eagerly wait for the Savior, the Lord Jesus Christ" (Phil. 3:20).

> *Therefore, beloved, looking forward to these things, be diligent to be found by Him in peace, without spot and blameless.*
>
> —2 PET. 3:14

Three

CHRIST'S GREATEST
PROPHETIC DISCOURSE

Other than the book of Revelation, the largest and most important prophetic portion of the New Testament is Matthew 24—25, known as *the Olivet Discourse.* It is the second-longest message of Christ recorded in Scripture. The only longer one, the Sermon on the Mount (Matthew 5—7), was a public sermon given to multitudes in Galilee near the beginning of Christ's earthly ministry. By contrast, the Olivet Discourse was a private message to His disciples in Jerusalem near the end of His earthly ministry. Our Lord spoke these words while seated directly across from the temple on the Mount of Olives, or as it is sometimes known, Mount Olivet (Matt. 24:3). So the popular name of this discourse is a reference to the place where it occurred.

From where they sat, Christ and the disciples could see the magnificent temple buildings. The temple was the most glorious of many grand building projects ordered by Herod the Great. The main temple edifice was a splendid structure. It was made of gleaming white marble with spectacular pure-gold decorations. Its eastern front (the side that faced where Jesus was sitting) was covered with gold plating that shone like a mirror in the morning sun. All that gold cast a brilliant glow that illuminated the whole western slope of the Mount of Olives and was visible for miles. It was by all accounts the most stunning and wonderful building in the world.

In fact, the opulence of the temple complex was what prompted the conversation that led to the Olivet Discourse. As Jesus left the temple mount on the way to the Mount of Olives, the disciples had expressed amazement at the grandeur of the temple. The parallel account in Luke 21:5 suggests they were marveling at the incredible wealth represented by the temple's fabulous decorations, which included many precious stones and other priceless ornaments, most of them donated by wealthy worshipers.

Jesus responded with a chilling prophecy: "Do you not see all these things? Assuredly, I say to you, not one stone shall be left here upon another, that shall not be thrown down" (Matt. 24:2). That prophecy echoed something else Christ had said to the Jewish leaders within the temple itself, probably just moments before: "Your house is left to you desolate" (Matt. 23:38).

The disciples must have wondered how anything as spectacular as the temple could be left "desolate." Christ's solemn prediction that not one stone of this glorious structure would be left standing amazed them even more. It undoubtedly confused them too. What He was now telling them was diametrically opposed to their Messianic expectations. They were sure He was the promised Messiah (cf. 16:16), and they fully expected Him to lead the nation to greater glory than ever—not to oversee its destruction.

Therefore, a short time later, as they sat across the Kidron Valley in clear view of the gleaming temple front, with the panorama of the whole temple mount stretched out before them, "The disciples came to Him privately, saying, 'Tell us, when will these things be? And what will be the sign of Your coming, and of the end of the age?'" (v. 3).

Jesus' reply was the longest answer He ever gave to any question recorded in the New Testament. The Olivet Discourse covers two long chapters in Matthew's Gospel. An abbreviated but parallel account fills most of Luke 21.

JEWISH MESSIANIC EXPECTATIONS

Understanding the disciples' questions requires an appreciation of how they and their countrymen envisioned Jesus' Messianic role. In their minds, the Messiah was chiefly a political figure who would deliver Israel from hostility and foreign occupation. All Israel believed that when their Messiah came, He would fully recover all that had been lost in their years of foreign exile and subsequent centuries of foreign oppression. Based on Old Testament promises in the Abrahamic and Davidic Covenants, they believed the Messiah would sort out and authenticate all the tribes and priestly lines of descent, reunify and purify the nation, and reestablish the Davidic throne in Jerusalem and bless the nation with a glory that was unprecedented and unimaginable. The disciples' expectation was no different. If anything, they regarded these things as nearer than most in Israel, because they already knew with certainty that Jesus was the Christ, the Anointed One whom the Old Testament prophecies foretold. So they thought they were on the very threshold of seeing His earthly kingdom established.

There is no better illustration of this expectation than the hymn of praise given by Zacharias, the father of John the Baptist. Realizing the forerunner of the Messiah had just been born, Zacharias anticipated the soon coming of Israel's Deliverer, and he recited the Messianic promises of the Abrahamic and Davidic Covenants in a hymn of praise to God:

> *Blessed is the Lord God of Israel, for He has visited and redeemed His people, and has raised up a horn of salvation for us in the house of His servant David, as He spoke by the mouth of His holy prophets, who have been since the world began, that we should be saved from our enemies and from the hand of all who hate us, to perform the mercy promised to our fathers and to remember His holy covenant, the oath which He swore to our father Abraham: to grant us that we, being delivered from the hand of our enemies, might serve Him without fear, in holiness and righteousness before Him all the days of our life.*
>
> LUKE 1:68-75

That hymn summed up the Old Testament's Messianic promise and Israel's hope: God visiting Israel for redemption, with the Savior and King in the Davidic line (2 Sam. 7:12-16; 1 Chron. 17:11-14; Ps. 89:27-37)—delivering the people from their enemies and making Israel the seat of His worldwide rulership. Messiah would also fulfill all of God's promises to Abraham—including blessing, protection, and possession of their land and victory over their enemies forever (Gen. 12:1-3; 15:18-21; 22:16-18). Zacharias believed all those promises would be immediately fulfilled with the coming of the Messiah, and he therefore anticipated the soon arrival of the promised kingdom of light and peace (Isa. 9:2-7; cf. Luke 2:25-32, 36-38).

Obviously, Zacharias was by no means alone in hoping for the immediate fulfillment of these things. Israel was at that time in the grip of Roman rule. The Roman Empire was at its peak, and Israel lay just inside the eastern edge of that vast empire. The Davidic throne had fallen hundreds of years before, and hopes of reviving it apart from the Messiah's supernatural intervention were by then completely nil. The only monarchy wielding power in the region during the disciples' lifetime was the Herodian dynasty, and even that was only by Rome's consent. Worse, the Herods themselves were also foreign rulers. They were most likely Idumeans—descendants of the Edomites, who were the offspring of Esau. The Edomites had long been uneasy neighbors and often bitter enemies of the Israelites (going back to the time of the Exodus, when the Edomites refused Israel passage through their land, Num. 20). So Israel was in effect governed by multiple layers of her own adversaries.

Furthermore, citizens of Israel were required to pay taxes to Rome, and those taxes went to pay for the occupation armies—Israel's chief oppressors! Understandably, most Israelites bitterly resented having to pay such a tax to Caesar (cf. Mark 12:13-17).

To make matters worse, Roman rule was often deliberately oppressive—and of all the regions in the vast empire, Israel became a singular target of Roman brutality. Unlike other countries under Roman rule, Israel's national identity was defined by a covenant relationship with Jehovah. For that reason, Roman polytheism (emperor worship in particular) found virtually no following among the Israelites. Roman governors therefore viewed monotheistic Judaism as inherently seditious. Meanwhile, Jewish zealots did everything they could to foster anti-Roman rebellion among their people. So political tensions ran high at this time, spurred by both Roman atrocities (cf. Luke 13:1) and violent Jewish insurrections (cf. Mark 15:7).

Because of Israel's national covenant with Jehovah, foreign rulers such as Herod and the Romans were perceived not merely as political enemies, but also as a shameful spiritual blight on the nation, signifying God's own displeasure with His people. Rome's occupation in Israel therefore posed a huge dilemma for Judaism. (This explains why some Jews had such a deep sense of national pride that they would not even concede the *fact* of Rome's dominion: "We are Abraham's descendants, and have never been in bondage to anyone. How can you say, 'You will be made free'?"— John 8:33). Every faithful heart in Israel longed for Rome to be overthrown so the nation could *truly* be free again. And they believed the Old Testament Messianic prophecies spoke of One who would suddenly appear and set all such things right, after which He would reestablish the throne of David on earth, ruling over all the other kingdoms of the world forever.

OLD TESTAMENT MESSIANIC PROPHECIES

Given the political climate, it is easy to see why the Jews were desperate for their Messiah to appear soon. But that is only one reason why Messianic expectation ran so high in Jesus' day. Old Testament prophecies also seemed to suggest that His coming *would* be soon (cf. Dan. 9:25). And those who were experts in Messianic prophecy were positive that when He finally appeared, the overthrow of Rome would be at the top of His agenda.

The heightened Messianic expectation among those who knew the Scriptures was the chief reason such great multitudes were willing to go into the wilderness to hear John the Baptist, and later

Christ (Matt. 3:4-6; Luke 5:15-16; 12:1). They believed the prophets had promised a conquering champion who would lead them. They expected not a suffering servant who would die, but a triumphant Messiah who would establish never-ending peace and prosperity in Israel and over all the world. And they would go to any length to find someone qualified to point the way to such a Deliverer.

The disciples clearly had similar expectations. No doubt when they read the Old Testament's Messianic promises, they had every expectation that Christ would soon bring them *all* to pass. They read, for example, Isaiah 9:6-7:

> *For unto us a Child is born, unto us a Son is given; and the gov-*
> *ernment will be upon His shoulder. And His name will be called*
> *Wonderful, Counselor, Mighty God, Everlasting Father, Prince of*
> *Peace. Of the increase of His government and peace there will be no*
> *end, upon the throne of David and over His kingdom, to order it and*
> *establish it with judgment and justice from that time forward, even*
> *forever. The zeal of the LORD of hosts will perform this.*

They knew verse 6 had been fulfilled in the birth of Christ. Naturally, they fully expected that Christ would also soon establish the perfect kingdom predicted in verse 7.

They no doubt clung to the triumphant promise in Jeremiah 23:5-6: "'Behold, the days are coming,' says the LORD, 'That I will raise to David a Branch of righteousness; a King shall reign and prosper, and execute judgment and righteousness in the earth. In His days Judah will be saved, and Israel will dwell safely.'" Having found Christ and *knowing* He was that promised Branch, they fully expected Him to fulfill the promise of an earthly kingdom in their lifetime.

What they did not see is that Bible prophecy sometimes compresses near and far events in contiguous prophetic statements—as when Christ stopped reading in the middle of Isaiah 61:2 and declared the passage fulfilled that very day in the Galileans' ears

(Luke 4:17-21). The phrase in Isaiah 61 that immediately follows Jesus' stopping-point is a prophecy about the day of God's vengeance (v. 2b). That part of the prophecy clearly has not yet been fulfilled.

From our perspective, it is easy to see that *many* of the Old Testament's Messianic prophecies juxtaposed events related to His first coming with prophecies that will not be fulfilled until He returns. But the distinction between the two advents was not so clear for the disciples.

THE DISCIPLES' IMMEDIATE MESSIANIC HOPES

It is obvious that Jesus' many prophecies about His own suffering and death had not fully registered with the disciples. They either ignored, doubted, rationalized, or spiritualized all those sayings to make them fit their own eschatalogical expectations. The Messianic relevance of many Old Testament prophecies such as Psalm 22 and Isaiah 53 remained unclear to them until after His resurrection (cf. Luke 24:25-32). Therefore, even as the time of His crucifixion approached, they remained dull to the agony He faced, despite all He had said about it. They were still looking for Jesus to emerge as the conquering Messiah all Israel hoped for—and they were convinced it would occur very soon.

The events immediately preceding the Olivet Discourse took place on Wednesday of Passion Week. Christ had entered the city only a few days before, cheered on by the enthusiastic adulation of large crowds. Practically the whole city had praised Him with loud shouts of "Hosanna" and had spread palm branches and even their own garments in His path (Matt. 21:8-11). To the disciples, it must have seemed that the kingdom was virtually His for the asking. As far as they were concerned, the reestablishment of David's throne and sovereignty was the next item on the eschatological calendar. As Luke 19:11 says, "They thought the kingdom of God would appear immediately."

So when Jesus predicted the utter demolition of the temple, the disciples were astonished. The temple was the very centerpiece and most visible remainder of Israel's national glory. Why would Israel's Messiah ever permit such a travesty against the nation? Hadn't He come to establish the kingdom in all its glory? Why would He foretell the *destruction* of Israel's glory? Could He not simply defeat Israel's enemies, take His rightful throne, and fulfill all those Old Testament promises of redemption, blessing, protection, peace, and prosperity? The destruction of the temple made no sense at all to the disciples (cf. John 2:20). What Jesus was predicting simply did not fit with their expectations of the Messiah.

That is the dilemma that led them to raise the questions of Matthew 24:3: "Tell us, when will these things be? And what will be the sign of Your coming, and of the end of the age?"

Keep in mind that the disciples were probably still flushed with euphoria over the public reception of Christ at His triumphal entry. They undoubtedly thought that was merely a prelude to an even greater triumph just on the horizon, when Christ would ascend His throne. He had not yet told them (as He would the following night) that He was going to return to the Father (John 14:2; 16:16). So at this point they would have had no concept of a "Second Coming" for the Messiah. The expression "Your coming" was a reference to His coming in triumph as Israel's Messiah—His ascendancy to the throne. The prophet Malachi had said Israel's Messiah would come suddeny to His temple as the Messenger of the covenant (Malachi 3:1)—that is, to fulfill all the covenant promises. But Jesus was predicting the temple's destruction. They no doubt were struggling to put all these prophecies together.

Since they no doubt assumed all the prophecies related to the Messiah's coming would occur in one unbroken sequence of events, they would have expected the final stages of the Messiah's work to unfold quickly. As far as they knew, all He had to do was defeat His enemies and establish His throne. That, according to the prophets, He would do by supernatural power ("He shall strike the earth with the rod of His mouth, and with the breath of His lips He shall slay the wicked," Isa. 11:4). Once everything began, the disciples believed, it would all occur with an astonishing swiftness. They may have been thinking the long-promised kingdom would become a reality before their eyes within a matter of days.[1]

But if Jesus was now telling them that something else must occur *before* He ascended His throne—especially something as catastrophic as the destruction of the temple—they wanted to know when these things would happen and what signs they should look for. So at the first opportunity they privately asked for an explanation of His remarks.

THE MESSIAH'S OWN PROPHETIC PROMISES

Whether they fully realized it or not, the disciples were actually raising multiple questions in Matthew 24:3. "When will these things be?" refers to the destruction of the temple and the events surrounding that catastrophe. "What will be the sign of Your coming, and of the end of the age?" deals with a larger eschatological subject—the question of how Christ's victorious coming as Israel's Messiah fits into the whole prophetic timetable.

As we shall see in chapters to come, Jesus' answers by no means erased all the mystery from those questions. The interpretation of the Olivet Discourse is no easy undertaking.

History records that the literal destruction of the temple took place in A.D. 70, when Roman armies under the command of Titus laid the whole city of Jerusalem waste. The Romans attacked the temple mount in particular, setting fires in the main temple structure that became so hot, the stones of the buildings crumbled. They then sifted the rubble to extract all the precious metals and gemstones and shoveled the remains of the temple into the surrounding valleys. So Jesus' words about the destruction of the temple were fulfilled to the letter. Not one stone was left standing atop another.[2] Josephus recorded that when the Roman army was through with it, the temple area looked like a wilderness that had never even been inhabited.

Many of Jesus' predictions about persecution and affliction

seem to anticipate that time with uncanny accuracy. But a closer look at the whole discourse reveals that the most important aspects of His prophecy were *not* fulfilled in the destruction of Jerusalem in A.D. 70. These unfulfilled elements include His own return and the gathering of the elect, described in verses 30-31: "The sign of the Son of Man will appear in heaven, and then all the tribes of the earth will mourn, and they will see the Son of Man coming on the clouds of heaven with power and great glory. And He will send His angels with a great sound of a trumpet, and they will gather together His elect from the four winds, from one end of heaven to the other."

Notice, moreover, that the great tribulation Christ described involves cataclysm and suffering on a global and cosmic scale (vv. 29-30)—not a local holocaust in Jerusalem only. Furthermore, He expressly foretold a time of distress and hardship that would be unique in all the world's history (v. 21)—not like the siege of Jerusalem in A.D. 70, which, though it indeed meant severe affliction, suffering, and widespread death for many people in that time, has been superseded by scores of far-worse calamities and holocausts in the centuries that have followed—including the systematic executions of millions of Jews by Hitler and Stalin in the twentieth century. The destruction of Jerusalem was indeed a great disaster, but in no sense can it accurately be said that the Roman siege of Jerusalem fulfilled the prophecy of "great tribulation, such as has not been since the beginning of the world until this time, no, nor ever shall be" (v. 21). Major aspects of Jesus' discourse therefore clearly await future fulfillment.

The only reasonable conclusion is that Jesus' prophecies in Matthew 24 are like the Old Testament Messianic prophecies that juxtaposed near-at-hand and far-off events in one context. In fact, such a conclusion seems unavoidable if we want to avert the error of those who deny the bodily return of Christ. After all, the destruction of the temple foretold in verse 2 was fulfilled by the Roman army in A.D. 70, but the cosmic signs accompanying the return of Christ described in verses 29-31 quite obviously still pertain to the future.

Furthermore, some of Jesus' words in the Olivet Discourse, like other prophetic passages in Scripture, appear to contain a kind of eschatological double entendre in which a prophecy at first glance appears to be fulfilled or partially fulfilled by one event, but a closer look reveals that an even greater or more precise fulfillment lies further off in the future.

In this very context, for example, Christ mentions "'the 'abomination of desolation,' spoken of by Daniel the prophet" (v. 15). He was referring to Daniel 11:31: "They shall defile the sanctuary fortress; then they shall take away the daily sacrifice, and place there the abomination of desolation." In its historical context, Daniel's prophecy seems to have been completely fulfilled by events that took place under the reign of Antiochus Epiphanes, a Seleucid king who conquered Jerusalem in the second century B.C., declared an end to the Jews' sacrifices, and defiled the temple by sacrificing a pig on the altar and setting up a statue of Zeus in the Holy Place. Those events precipitated the Maccabean revolt, which occurred more than a century before Christ. But here He clearly spoke of "the abomination of desolation" as something yet future, an abomination that exceeded even the deliberate blasphemy of Antiochus Epiphanes. Daniel's "abomination of desolation" therefore must have referred to a yet-future, greater reality than the blasphemy of Antiochus, which initially seemed to be its fulfillment.

In a similar way Christ's warnings about false messiahs, wars, rumors of wars, famines, pestilences, and earthquakes may have seemed to foretell what took place on a limited scale during the siege of Jerusalem in A.D. 70, but many clues throughout this context suggest that the precise and final fulfillment of these prophecies awaits a yet-future cataclysm that will be worldwide rather than local, and apocalyptic rather than merely historic.

What are those clues? For one thing, the disciples' more important question had to do with "the end of the age" (v. 3). Jesus Himself had used the phrase in two of His parables—the parable of the tares (Matt. 13:39) and the parable of the dragnet (13:49). In both places He spoke of the final judgment of the wicked. He also used the phrase in the promise that accompanied His Great Commission: "I am with you always, even to the end of the age" (Matt. 28:20). So it was clearly a reference to the end of the eschatological age, not merely the events leading up to the last days of the temple in Jerusalem.

But notice also that Christ's only explicit remarks about the destruction of the temple are those recorded in verse 2, as Jesus and the disciples were departing from the temple (v. 1). In the Olivet Discourse itself He makes no clear reference to the events of A.D. 70. His entire reply is an extended answer to the more important question about the signs of His coming and the end of the age. Virtually ignoring their initial question, He said nothing whatsoever about when the destruction of Jerusalem would occur. That is because those events were not really germane to the end of the age. They were merely a foretaste of the greater judgment that would accompany His return, previews of what is to come ultimately.

Preterists object to this interpretation of the Olivet Discourse. Invariably they point to Christ's words in verse 34 ("Assuredly, I say to you, this generation will by no means pass away till all these things take place"). They insist that this proves Christ was speaking about events that would take place within about forty years, which would mean the events of A.D. 70 *must* be the fulfillment of these prophecies.

But if verse 34 is to be understood with such wooden literalness, the rest of the Olivet Discourse must be spiritualized or otherwise interpreted figuratively in order to explain how Christ's prophecies could all have been fulfilled by A.D. 70 without His returning bodily to earth.

As we noted in the introduction to this book, hyper-preterists handle this dilemma by flatly denying the bodily return of Christ, the resurrection of the dead, and other vital Christian doctrines—all because they insist on a too-literal interpretation of Matthew 24:34. Most preterists take a less extreme position and manage to avoid such serious heresy, but they must ultimately do so by acknowledging that key prophecies in the Olivet Discourse are yet-future events. So in essence they ultimately depart from and nullify the strict literal sense of Matthew 24:34 anyway.

It seems more sensible and more consistent, therefore, to take a futurist approach with respect to the Olivet Discourse—to interpret the entire discourse as a prophetic picture of a "generation" and events that would take place long after the destruction of Jerusalem in A.D. 70. These are events that will immediately precede Christ's coming to establish His kingdom, and therefore they are events that are yet future even today. That seems to be the sense conveyed by the passage itself (e.g., vv. 29-31), and it is the interpretation I believe the text demands.

So as we delve into a verse-by-verse study of the discourse in the chapters that follow, that is the approach we will be taking. These verses describe the signs of Christ's coming and the end of the age. They are as relevant to our future as they were to those believers in the earliest days of the Christian era. They speak of a time yet future when Christ will return bodily to earth. And therefore they set forth the hope of every true believer. Prepare your heart for a rich feast as we dig into the passage.

four

BIRTH PANGS

The central message of Christ's Olivet Discourse is a twofold admonition. First, our Lord is warning that before He returns, the world will become more and more hostile to the people of God. And second, He is urging people to be prepared for His coming and the judgments that are associated with it.

Those themes dominate the whole discourse, including the parables at the end. Specific elements of Christ's prophecies may be difficult to comprehend fully, but the basic thrust is impossible to miss: The world's hostility to Christ will not diminish but will increase dramatically (Matt. 24:4-20). The final result will be a time of tribulation like none the world has ever known (vv. 21-29). And when Christ finally returns at the end of those days of tribulation, no one will miss His coming, and no enemy will escape His retribution (vv. 30-51).

Nowhere does our Lord suggest the kind of prophetic scenario postmillennialists envision, where the church's evangelistic and social efforts eventually win the world for Christ and establish His earthly kingdom, thereby preparing the way for His return. (It is no wonder so many postmillennialists favor the preterist interpretation of the Olivet Discourse. By relegating the significance of this passage to a long-gone, first-century event, they eliminate the problem of reconciling the decidedly "pessimistic" prophecies of this discourse with their "optimistic" view of the world's future.)[1]

Remember, the Olivet Discourse was given to a group of disciples who "thought the kingdom of God would appear immediately" (Luke 19:11). Christ was making it clear to them that the earthly kingdom they hoped for belonged to the eschatological future. While He declined to set a precise time or date for these events (Matt. 24:36), He did outline many signs that would indicate the time was drawing near. And all those signs point to a time of tribulation unlike any other in the history of the world—a time so filled with suffering and affliction that if Christ did not intervene, everyone on earth would die (vv. 21-22).

The afflictions Christ outlines in Matthew 24 closely parallel the dreadful judgments described in Revelation 7—19. A comparison of the two passages reveals several unmistakable connections. Both passages describe a time of unprecedented affliction culminating in the glorious return of Christ. The only reasonable interpretation is that they both refer to the same cataclysmic period of distress and hardship. Revelation 7:14 refers to it as "the great tribulation," employing the definite article to signify that this is a specific eschatological period. Jesus likewise described this era as a time of "great tribulation, such as has not been since the beginning of the world until this time, no, nor ever shall be" (Matt. 24:21). He was quite obviously describing the same period of apocalyptic judgment depicted in detail in the apostle John's vision. The relationships between the two passages of Scripture will be apparent as we work through the Olivet Discourse.

THE TRIBULATION AND DANIEL'S SEVENTIETH WEEK

Comparing Scripture with Scripture, it becomes unmistakably clear that the Tribulation period Christ described in the Olivet Discourse is the same eschatological era signified by the last of seventy prophetic "weeks" referred to in Daniel 9:25-27:

> *"Know therefore and understand, that from the going forth of the command to restore and build Jerusalem until Messiah the Prince, there shall be seven weeks and sixty-two weeks; the street shall be built again, and the wall, even in troublesome times. And after the sixty-two weeks Messiah shall be cut off, but not for Himself; and*

the people of the prince who is to come shall destroy the city and the sanctuary. The end of it shall be with a flood, and till the end of the war desolations are determined. Then he shall confirm a covenant with many for one week; but in the middle of the week he shall bring an end to sacrifice and offering. And on the wing of abominations shall be one who makes desolate, even until the consummation, which is determined, is poured out on the desolate."

The "weeks" Daniel speaks of are actually seven-year periods. (The Hebrew word is *šabu̇·a,* literally "sevens.") Notice that Daniel says sixty-nine (seven plus sixty-two) of these seven-year periods (or 483 years) would elapse "from the going forth of the command to restore and build Jerusalem until Messiah the Prince."

"The command to restore and build Jerusalem" most likely refers to Artaxerxes' decree recorded in Nehemiah 2:1-8, which occurred in the month of Nisan in the twentieth year of Artaxexes' reign (Neh. 2:1). History places that decree approximately 450 years before the advent of Christ. So the sixty-nine prophetic weeks—483 years—may actually have been a precise figure that signified the exact day and year when Christ would enter Jerusalem in triumph. (This occurred in the month of Nisan too—on the first day of Passover week—probably in A.D. 30 or 33.)[2] Immediately afterward, Messiah was "cut off" (by crucifixion), just as Daniel prophesied. Thus Daniel's sixty-ninth prophetic week concluded.

Remember, however, that Daniel's prophecy covered *seventy* weeks (9:24). When does the seventieth week occur? Daniel recounts all seventy weeks without mentioning any gap between the sixty-ninth and seventieth weeks. In the sixty-ninth week, Messiah is "cut off" (v. 26). In the seventieth week, an evil "prince who is to come" makes a covenant, then interrupts the week with an act of abomination. This appears to be another instance where Old Testament prophecy juxtaposes near and far events. The sixty-nine weeks obviously began with the decree to rebuild Jerusalem and continued uninterrupted until Messiah was "cut off." But when we compare Daniel's description of the seventieth week with Christ's words in the Olivet Discourse, we discover that these passages actually refer to the same eschatalogical end-time period. In other words, Daniel's seventieth week *is* the Tribulation period Christ referred to. It belongs to the end of the age.

How do we know this? Notice carefully how Daniel describes the events of that seventieth week. "The prince who is to come . . . shall confirm a covenant with many for one week" (vv. 26-27). But something happens halfway through the seventieth week: "In the middle of the week he shall bring an end to sacrifice and offering. And on the wing of abominations shall be one who makes desolate" (v. 27). That quite clearly describes the very same "abomination of desolation" Jesus mentions in Matthew 24:15. Thus Daniel's seventieth week is expressly associated with the same events described in the Olivet Discourse. The seventieth week is none other than the seven-year period we refer to as "the Tribulation."

Numerous passages of Scripture suggest that this seven-year period comes in two halves. The first half will be a period of unbridled indulgence in sin for most of the world, but hardship and persecution for the people of God. Then suddenly, "in the middle of the week" (Dan. 9:27), the abomination of desolation occurs, and the rest of the week ushers in the most horrible era of tribulation and hardship in all of human history (Matt. 24:21). The second half of the week is measured several ways in Scripture: "forty-two months" (Rev. 11:2; 13:5); "one thousand two hundred and sixty days" (Rev. 11:3; 12:6); and "a time and times and half a time" (Dan. 7:25; Rev. 12:14). All those expressions signify a period of three and a half years' duration. It is the latter half of Daniel's final prophetic "week."

Students of Bible prophecy usually speak of the whole seven-year period as "the Tribulation" and reserve the expression "the *Great* Tribulation" for the second half of the "week." In the Olivet Discourse Christ Himself says "tribulation" will be one of the beginning sorrows (Matt. 24:9), but after mentioning "the 'abomination of desolation'" (v. 15), He uses the expression "great tribulation" (v. 21). So the abomination of desolation marks the key turning point of the Tribulation period. From that time on, things grow worse and worse, culminating finally in Christ's glorious appearing (Matt. 24:29-30).

Where Is the Church During the Tribulation?

One vital question must be addressed before we delve into the specifics of the Olivet Discourse: If our Lord is outlining this detailed series of events that will precede and portend His coming in glory—if a seven-year Tribulation period must happen *before* He returns to earth—then in what sense can we maintain the view that His coming is imminent (see Chapter 2 of this book)?

Scripture suggests that the Second Coming occurs in two stages—first the Rapture, when He comes *for* the saints and they are caught up to meet Him in the air (1 Thess. 4:14-17), and second, His return to earth, when He comes *with* His saints (Jude 14) to execute judgment against His enemies. Daniel's seventieth week must fall *between* those two events. That is the only scenario that reconciles the imminency of Christ's coming *for* His saints with the yet-unfulfilled signs that signal His final glorious return *with* the saints.

In other words, the entire church will be removed from the earth before the Tribulation begins. Scripture indicates that during Daniel's seventieth week, national Israel, not the church, will be the focus of God's earthly program. The whole Tribulation period is a prelude to the national redemption spoken of in Romans 11:26, when "all Israel will be saved, as it is written: 'The Deliverer will come out of Zion, and He will turn away ungodliness from Jacob.'" The Rapture—the removal of the church—signifies that "the fullness of the Gentiles has come in" (v. 25). And the onset of the Tribulation marks the start of the painful process by which national Israel will be grafted back into the olive tree (cf. v. 24).

Jeremiah 30:7 is a key text in understanding the nature of the Tribulation: "Alas! For that day is great, so that none is like it; and *it is the time of Jacob's trouble*, but he shall be saved out of it" (emphasis added). Clearly, the significance of the Tribulation pertains to ethnic and national Israel, not the church. Nowhere is the church mentioned in any of the Bible's descriptions of the Tribulation. In fact, the apostle John's description of heaven features twenty-four elders (Rev. 4:4). They represent the New Testament church, "elders" (*presbuteros* in the Greek text) being the same word used for officers in the church. The events associated with the Tribulation in Revelation do not even begin until chapter 6, after those elders were already seen in heaven.

Someone will point out that one of the recurring themes in the Tribulation prophecies throughout Scripture is that believers who live in that era will be severely persecuted for their faith. So if the church is taken to heaven *before* the Tribulation, where do these believers come from? The obvious answer is that they are believers who come to faith after the Rapture.

The Rapture is indeed imminent; it could occur at any time. The second stage of Christ's return—His coming in glory *with* the saints—is the event all the signs and warnings in the Olivet Discourse point to.

Some have asked why the Lord would warn people during New Testament times as He does in this message, when He knew they would never live to experience these terrible signs. Indeed, why include this in the Gospel account, where it has stood as a warning to the church in every generation? But a similar question could be asked about Isaiah's prophecy and his warnings about the Babylonian captivity (Isa. 39:6-7), which did not occur until *after* all the people of Isaiah's generation were dead. The message is given to be a warning to all about the consequences of sin—and it will stand as a specific warning to those who will actually experience the terrible judgment.

Now let's turn to the text of the Olivet Discourse itself and see what those signs are.

THE PAINS OF HARD LABOR

Christ begins His discourse with a long list of calamities He likens to the labor pains that precede childbirth:

Jesus answered and said to them: "Take heed that no one deceives you. For many will come in My name, saying, 'I am the Christ,' and will deceive many. And you will hear of wars and rumors of wars. See that you are not troubled; for all these things must come to pass, but the end is not yet. For nation will rise against nation, and kingdom against kingdom. And there will be famines, pestilences, and earthquakes in various places. All these are the beginning of sorrows."

—MATT. 24:4-8

The word "sorrows" in verse 8 is from the Greek term *ōdin*, which speaks of the travail and pain of childbirth. The afflictions Christ lists here are like birth pangs. At first they are relatively mild and infrequent, but then they come in relentless waves, faster and harder as the time approaches.

The imagery of birth pangs is fairly common in Jewish apocalyptic literature. The apostle Paul used a similar figure to describe the approach of the day of the Lord: "When they say, 'Peace and safety!' then sudden destruction comes upon them, as labor pains upon a pregnant woman. And they shall not escape" (1 Thess. 5:3).

As we noted above, the context indicates that these signs apply in a particular way to the Tribulation era. Yet these very evils (wars and rumors of wars, false christs, natural disasters, and persecution) are all afflictions that have characterized the whole of the Christian era. Similar features are present right now in varying degrees, and collectively they seem to be growing steadily worse and ever more prevalent, just like birth pangs.

That doesn't mean the era we are living in is the one Christ describes. But it *does* underscore the imminency of Christ's return for the church. The world in which we live is already ripe for the Tribulation. Elements like the birth-pang signs are already being felt. The present afflictions may merely be like Braxton-Hicks contractions—premature labor pains—but they nonetheless signify that the time for hard labor, and then delivery, is inevitable and quickly drawing near.

What are the birth pangs? Christ names six distinct signs.

False messiahs. "Take heed that no one deceives you. For many will come in My name, saying, 'I am the Christ,' and will deceive many" (vv. 4-5; cf. 2 Pet. 2:1-3; 2 Tim. 3:13). False messiahs are nothing new. There were plenty of false christs even before Jesus' time, and there have been multitudes of them throughout church history. Our own generation has produced numerous notorious false messiahs and religious deceivers. Sun Myung Moon, David Koresh, Jim Jones, Marshall Applewhite ("Do" of the infamous Heaven's Gate cult), and Charles Manson—these are just a handful of many notorious cult leaders who have claimed to be the incarnation of Christ in our lifetime. They are classic false messiahs, and they have already deceived many naive people.

Such deception during the Tribulation period will reach epidemic proportions. When the church is taken out of the world, deceivers and false religions will be able to work more freely and more persuasively than ever. In effect, the Holy Spirit will withdraw His restraining power, and all hell will break loose (2 Thess. 2:7-8).

Not only will the deceit be more powerful, but people will also be so lacking in discernment that they will be more vulnerable to the lies than ever. "God will send them strong delusion, that they should believe the lie" (2 Thess. 2:11). Except for the remnant who will be saved by God's sovereign intervention, everyone on earth during the Tribulation will be deceived by the lies of the false messiahs (cf. Matt. 24:24). In fact, overwhelming hostility toward the true Gospel will no doubt be one of the factors that makes the deceivers' lies so compelling. Yet, as is always the case, public opinion is no yardstick for measuring truth. Those who follow the public blindly will merely be all the more easily taken in by the lies of the deceivers.

Therefore Jesus warns the faithful remnant, "Take heed that no one deceives you" (v. 4). He uses a word that speaks of keeping one's eyes open, remaining watchful. We ought always to be on guard against religious deceivers, but this will become especially crucial for those living in the Tribulation, when deceit and false religion will virtually have free rein.

Again, not only will the number of false messiahs and deceivers increase, but so will the number of gullible people. Multitudes will be desperate to escape the afflictions of a quickly disintegrating world. False messiahs will seize the opportunity, promising various forms of deliverance to people yearning for a way of escape from the worsening Tribulation.

The epitome of all false prophets will come on the scene as a beast who arises from the earth (Rev. 13:11-18) with an amazing ability to work supernatural signs and wonders (or *appear* to do so convincingly). He has power to call down fire from heaven (v. 13) and the ability to animate lifeless objects (v. 15). By wielding such power, he will deceive most of the world. And this beast, referred to as "the false prophet" in Revelation 19:20 (cf. 16:13; 20:10), will employ his deceptive powers to get the world to follow *another* beast (Rev. 13:1-10). The other beast (often designated *the Beast* in distinction from his cohort, *the False Prophet)* becomes the object of worship in the False Prophet's religion (vv. 14-15). This Beast also emerges as the chief earthly adversary of Christ (19:19). Although the book of Revelation never expressly applies the title to him, most students of Bible prophecy associate the Beast with *the Antichrist* mentioned in 1 John 2:18; 4:3. He is the ultimate false christ.

Wars and rumors of wars. The end-times birth pangs will also include warfare and the threat of warfare on an unprecedented scale. "You will hear of wars and rumors of wars" (Matt. 24:6). The verb tense suggests continual action—literally, "you will be hearing." In other words, there will be constant talk of such things, some of it true ("wars"), and some mere hearsay ("rumors of wars"). The subject of war will dominate public discourse. This was largely the case from the beginning to the end of the twentieth century. The entire century was dominated by talk of war—world wars, cold wars, "military actions," civil wars, border conflicts, terrorism, and revolutions of various kinds. Even the term "peacekeeping mission" often turned out to be a euphemism for war.

There will doubtless be even more of the same in the Tribulation. Again, the analogy of labor pains suggests that the talk of war will steadily increase in frequency and intensity as the return of Christ approaches. Indeed, Scripture teaches that Christ will return in the middle of an enormous battle of unprecedented proportions, and the result of His appearing will be the greatest holocaust of bloodshed and carnage the world has ever seen (Rev. 19:19-21).

The onset of "wars and rumors of wars" is a necessary step leading to the return of Christ—just one more labor pain that signals the approaching delivery. All the talk of war may make it seem as if the end of the world has arrived, but it really only marks the beginning of the end: "See that you are not troubled; for all these things must come to pass, but the end is not yet" (Matt. 24:6).

Famines, pestilences, and earthquakes in various places. The onset of birth pangs will also bring about an unprecedented increase in natural disasters. The parallel verse in Luke 21:11 adds a couple of additional details: "There will be great earthquakes in various places, and famines and pestilences; and there will be fearful sights and great signs from heaven." The "signs from heaven" Luke mentions could include asteroids, debris from a comet, or similar cosmic disasters. The prophet Joel repeatedly spoke about the darkening of the sun and moon (2:10, 31; 3:15; cf. Isa. 13:10; Rev. 6:12), suggesting that these cosmic signs will eventually reach epic proportions as the pains of labor become more intense.

This third sign of birth pangs makes it inescapably clear that the birth-pang afflictions are a display of God's judgment. Because religious deception and war involve deliberate human acts, some might be reluctant to conclude that they represent any kind of divine judgment. Pestilences and famines are often immediate *consequences* of sin, so some might also suggest that God has no hand in bringing these about. But earthquakes and cosmic catastrophes are direct, undeniable acts of God. (Scripture does teach that religious deception and war, as well as all the natural consequences of human sin, often represent divine judgment. See 2 Thess. 2:11-12; Joel 3:9-10.) So *all* the birth-pang signs are expressions of divine judgment. God exercises sovereign, providential control over all such afflictions and catastrophes, and their sudden, dramatic increase will signify that He is beginning to pour out His judgment on the earth.

The global increase in disease, hunger, and natural disasters will torment humanity. It will seem as if the world itself is beginning to disintegrate. And in a sense that is exactly what will be happening. God will withdraw His providential mercy (cf. Lam. 3:22). He will unleash the full consequences of sin. And He will allow the full repercussions of the curse to be felt in the natural disasters that occur. All the destructive forces of evil will be set loose.

Still, these are merely birth pangs, the onset of labor, "the beginning of sorrows" (Matt. 24:8). Things are going to get worse. These birth pangs bring "tribulation." "*Great* tribulation" is yet to come. And the state of fear and foreboding that will grip an unbelieving world in those indescribable days will be terrifying indeed.

Again, John's account in the book of Revelation exactly parallels what Christ predicts here. In John's vision, when Christ breaks the fourth seal of earth's title deed, death and Hades are unleashed. "And power was given to them [Death and Hades] over a fourth of the earth, to kill with sword, with hunger, with death, and by the beasts of the earth" (6:8). These correspond exactly to the famines and pestilences of Matthew 24:7.

Then, at the breaking of the sixth seal, a massive earthquake—perhaps a series of major earthquakes along the edges of the earth's tectonic plates—wreaks global havoc. And that elevates the worldwide sense of panic and dread to greater proportions than ever:

I looked when He opened the sixth seal, and behold, there was a great earthquake; and the sun became black as sackcloth of hair, and the moon became like blood. And the stars of heaven fell to the earth, as a fig tree drops its late figs when it is shaken by a mighty wind. Then the sky receded as a scroll when it is rolled up, and every mountain and island was moved out of its place. And the kings of the earth, the great men, the rich men, the commanders, the mighty men, every slave and every free man, hid themselves in the caves and in the rocks of the mountains.

—6:12-15

That pictures global catastrophe on a scale unprecedented since Noah's flood. It includes the "earthquakes in various places" of Matthew 24:7 as well as the fearful cosmic phenomena described in the parallel passage of Luke 21:11.

But again, according to Christ in Matthew 24:8, "All these are [only] the beginning of sorrows."

The book of Revelation explains what Christ means by this. John goes on to describe how the seventh seal is broken, and seven angels appear before God. Each is handed a trumpet, signifying God's judgment. Incense is given to God in a golden censer, and John says that incense represents the prayers of the saints. To be precise, these are prayers for God to rise up and enact justice against His enemies (Rev. 8:3-4).

An angel takes the censer, fills it with fire from the altar, and throws it to earth, signifying that those prayers for justice have been heard, and God's judgment is about to fall. Then the angels with the trumpets prepare themselves to sound (vv. 5-6). What happens next is frightening:

The first angel sounded: And hail and fire followed, mingled with blood, and they were thrown to the earth. And a third of the trees were burned up, and all green grass was burned up.

Then the second angel sounded: And something like a great mountain burning with fire was thrown into the sea, and a third of the sea became blood. And a third of the living creatures in the sea died, and a third of the ships were destroyed.

Then the third angel sounded: And a great star fell from heaven, burning like a torch, and it fell on a third of the rivers and on the springs of water. The name of the star is Wormwood. A third of the waters became wormwood, and many men died from the water, because it was made bitter.

> *Then the fourth angel sounded: And a third of the sun was struck, a third of the moon, and a third of the stars, so that a third of them were darkened. A third of the day did not shine, and likewise the night.*
>
> *And I looked, and I heard an angel flying through the midst of heaven, saying with a loud voice, "Woe, woe, woe to the inhabitants of the earth, because of the remaining blasts of the trumpet of the three angels who are about to sound!"*
>
> —REV. 8:7-13

So even massive catastrophes such as those are *still* merely the prelude to an even greater judgment yet to come. Amazingly, Revelation 16 describes an earthquake far worse than the one in Revelation 6. The birth pangs continue to get worse, "but the end is not yet" (Matt. 24:6).

Persecution of the righteous. Those who do come to faith during the Tribulation period will pay a tremendous price in terms of suffering and persecution. Jesus says, "Then they will deliver you up to tribulation and kill you, and you will be hated by all nations for My name's sake" (v. 9). The Greek verb translated "will deliver" is *paradidomi* and was often used to speak of arrest and imprisonment. It is the very word used to describe the imprisonment of John the Baptist in Matthew 4:12 ("John had been put in prison"). It is also translated "betrayed" in Matthew 10:4, 17:22, and 20:18, describing Judas' act of treachery against Christ. In fact, the same word is employed just a verse later right here in the Olivet Discourse. In Matthew 24:10 it is again translated "betrayed," suggesting that some of the persecution Jesus is describing here will be instigated by people who have pretended to be friendly to the faith.

Betrayal and imprisonment are not the only, nor by any means the worst, persecutions believers will face. Many will be killed for their faith. *All* will be hated "by all nations" on account of Christ. A parallel passage in Mark suggests that the persecutors of the faithful will include earthly governments: "But watch out for yourselves, for they will deliver you up to councils, and you will be beaten in the synagogues. You will be brought before rulers and kings for My sake, for a testimony to them" (Mark 13:9). "Councils" seem to represent Gentile courts, and "synagogues" obviously speak of Jewish authorities. Persecution will come from both groups, and "rulers and kings" will lend their support.

The world's persecution of believers is an expression of blind hatred toward God. John's account of the earthquake in Revelation 6:15-17 suggests that the people of earth *know* these birth-pang signs are harbingers of the judgment of God, and yet they only steel their hearts against Him all the more:

> *The kings of the earth, the great men, the rich men, the commanders, the mighty men, every slave and every free man, hid themselves in the caves and in the rocks of the mountains, and said to the mountains and rocks, "Fall on us and hide us from the face of Him who sits on the throne and from the wrath of the Lamb! For the great day of His wrath has come, and who is able to stand?"*

With full knowledge that God's judgment is the source of their afflictions, they vainly try to hide from Him and continue in their blind hatred of Him, rather than repenting of their own unrighteousness. And since they cannot strike back at God, they lash out at His people.

With the restraining hand of God withdrawn to let wickedness flourish unhindered, Satan will be turned loose to have his diabolical way with the world. The governments of earth, in collusion with one another out of sheer hatred for God, will throw off His moral law and give people free rein in the expression of their unrighteousness. And with God-hating people given unprecedented latitude to pursue their evil ambitions, believers will suffer persecution as never before.

Again, the tribulations foretold in the book of Revelation correspond precisely to Jesus' words here. The apostle John describes how when the fifth seal of the scroll was broken, he saw the souls of martyred saints under the heavenly altar, crying out to God for justice. "And they cried with a loud voice, saying, 'How long, O

Lord, holy and true, until You judge and avenge our blood on those who dwell on the earth?'" (Rev. 6:10).

To some it may seem as if God is unresponsive to the cries of these martyrs. They plead with Him to stop the bloodshed, spare His people from further slaughter, and act against the evildoers. But notice what they are told: "It was said to them that they should rest a little while longer, until both the number of their fellow servants and their brethren, who would be killed as they were, was completed" (v. 11; cf. 11:7; 13:7; 17:6).

At first glance that reply may seem cold and indifferent. But think about its implications. It suggests that there is a fixed number of saints to be martyred. While the suffering is going on, it may seem that the torrent of martyrdoms has no end. But there *is* an end to the suffering, and that end is already fixed by God Himself. He has established a boundary beyond which the forces of evil will never be permitted to work (cf. Matt. 24:22).

Obviously, then, God also has a purpose in permitting the martyrdom of so many people. We can take great encouragement in this because it demonstrates that even when things on earth seem most out of control, when it finally seems as if Satan and the forces of evil have actually got the upper hand, God is nonetheless still in control. He will allow evil workers to go so far and then no further.

Moreover, if God has a purpose in permitting His people to suffer so badly, then we know it is a *good* purpose, because all His purposes are good and righteous and perfect. Therefore, these martyrdoms are not for nothing. They fulfill some good purpose; and even though *what* that purpose is may be a mystery to those who are suffering, they can rest in the promise that God will lovingly use even trials as severe as these for His people's ultimate good (Rom. 8:28).

And the day will come when God's purposes in permitting such things will be made clear to us. When that occurs, we will confess, along with the martyrs themselves, that God deserves our highest praise for all He has done. The apostle John even saw this come to pass in his vision. In the very next chapter he describes "a great multitude which no one could number, of all nations, tribes, peoples, and tongues, standing before the throne and before the Lamb, clothed with white robes, with palm branches in their hands, and crying out with a loud voice, saying, 'Salvation belongs to our God who sits on the throne, and to the Lamb!'" (Rev. 7:9-10).

Who are these people? One of the elders rhetorically asked the apostle John that very question. John says, "And I said to him, 'Sir, you know.' So he said to me, 'These are the ones who come out of the great tribulation, and washed their robes and made them white in the blood of the Lamb'" (v. 14).

In other words, even the martyrs themselves, victims of the worst atrocities ever perpetrated by the forces of evil, will ultimately glorify God in heaven for His goodness to them. That should be a great encouragement in the midst of our relatively petty trials here and now—because it means the day is coming when we will recognize the wisdom and goodness of God even in allowing the bad things that happen to us. When we finally see those trials from heaven's perspective, we will praise God for them.

In the midst of our tribulations, however, it is far too easy to be distracted by our own suffering and pain, to take our eyes off our sovereign God, to forget that He promises to work all things for our good, and to become so obsessed with the trials themselves that we grow discouraged. That sort of discouragement undermines faith itself, as is revealed in the next of the birth-pang signs.

Defection of false believers. The hardships of the Tribulation will give rise to so much persecution and such a widespread contempt for believers that many who profess love for Christ, people who think of themselves as friends to the truth, will break under the strain. They will fall away from the faith, turn against other believers, and even attack and twist the truth itself, steering people *away* from the saving Gospel of Christ after having posed as His followers. Thus the already tiny remnant of believers will be torn asunder by turncoats and betrayers. Jesus describes this birth-pang: "And then many will be offended, will betray one another, and will hate one another. Then many false prophets will rise up and deceive many. And because lawlessness will abound, the love of many will grow cold. But he who endures to the end shall be saved" (Matt. 24:10-13).

These defectors are not genuine believers who fall away. They are people who perhaps have an intellectual interest in Christianity, who are drawn to Christ in an outward sense only. They identify with Him verbally and superficially. They pretend to love Him. By all outward appearances they seem like true believers. But their faith stops short of reality. They hold something back and entertain secret misgivings about Christ—which is really the same kind of clandestine contempt for Him Judas had. In some sense they stop short of true and full commitment to Him. And as the persecution and fear intensify, they simply cannot hold out. As believers are hated, arrested, and killed for Christ's sake, these pseudo-followers defect, thus proving that they never truly belonged to Him. "They went out from us, but they were not of us; for if they had been of us, they would have continued with us; but they went out that they might be made manifest, that none of them were of us" (1 John 2:19).

Worse yet, many of these defectors will become the chief persecutors of God's people. And they will do so in the most abominable and nefarious ways. "Brother will betray brother to death, and a father his child; and children will rise up against parents and cause them to be put to death" (Mark 13:12; cf. Luke 21:16).

Meanwhile, those who are truly God's people *will* endure despite the severity of the persecution. In Revelation John pictures 144,000 believers as having been sealed with a sign in their foreheads. And their sealing takes place *before* the most serious trials come. So the seal signifies beforehand that these people belong to God (Rev. 7:2-8).[3] Notice, then, that these people are not granted acceptance from God *because* of their endurance; rather, their endurance is proof that they are among the ones who are saved.

The context suggests three reasons why everyone but genuine believers will defect from the faith:

• *The cost will be too high* (Matt. 24:9-10). Hangers-on may at first have selfish or merely altruistic reasons for identifying with the people of God. But the cost of professing loyalty to Christ will soon prove too high for them, for they themselves will become targets of persecution, and that will drive them away. They are classic examples of what Christ illustrated with the shallow-soil seedling, "who hears the word and immediately receives it with joy; yet he has no root in himself, but endures only for a while. For when tribulation or persecution arises because of the word, immediately he stumbles" (Matt. 13:20-21). But as Jesus Himself told some too-eager followers who were not really prepared to commit all to Him, "No one, having put his hand to the plow, and looking back, is fit for the kingdom of God" (Luke 9:62).

• *The deception will be too convincing.* The defection of professing believers will give rise to a whole new wave of false prophets. They may rise mostly from the ranks of the defectors themselves. "Then many false prophets will rise up and deceive many" (Matt. 24:11). Perhaps because they once professed loyalty to Christ, these false prophets will be particularly effective in their deception and will draw many away with them.

• *The lure of sin will be too attractive.* "Because lawlessness will abound, the love of many will grow cold" (v. 12). Iniquity will be rife. People will no longer try to hide their sins. Sin will be flaunted openly (as is happening increasingly even today). And since love is what fulfills the moral law of God (Rom. 13:8-10; Gal. 5:14; Jas. 2:8), the abundance of immorality will have a chilling effect on genuine love. People will therefore be susceptible to the enticements of sin like never before, and many shallow-rooted people who once claimed friendship with Christ will demonstrate that they are actually friends of the world instead (cf. Jas. 4:4).

Persecution is promised for—and endurance is demanded from—every genuine believer. "Yes, and all who desire to live godly in Christ Jesus will suffer persecution" (2 Tim. 3:12). "A disciple is not above his teacher, nor a servant above his master. It is enough for a disciple that he be like his teacher, and a servant like his master. If they have called the master of the house Beelzebub, how much more will they call those of his household!" (Matt. 10:24-25).

The true believer must be willing to suffer as Christ suffered. "And he who does not take his cross and follow after Me is not worthy of Me" (Matt. 10:38).

But true believers *will* endure, because God Himself guarantees their endurance. "I will put My fear in their hearts so that they will not depart from Me" (Jer. 32:40). They are "are kept by the power of God through faith for salvation" (1 Pet. 1:5). Scripture is full of statements that promise the perseverance of all genuine believers. For example, Jesus said, "My sheep hear My voice, and I know them, and they follow Me. And I give them eternal life, and they shall never perish; neither shall anyone snatch them out of My hand" (John 10:27-28).

People who *are* plucked away from their professions of faith by wily deceivers are no exception to that promise. Their departure is irrefutable proof that their "faith" was never real to begin with (1 John 2:19).

"But he who endures to the end shall be saved" (Matt. 24:13). Despite the high cost of discipleship, no matter the deception of false prophets, and regardless of the enticement of sin, *nothing* can cause true believers to renounce Christ. Christ Himself protects them from such defection.

The Gospel proclaimed to the whole world. The final birth-pang sign is markedly different in character from all the others: "And this gospel of the kingdom will be preached in all the world as a witness to all the nations, and then the end will come" (v. 14). In the midst of so much deception—false messiahs, false teachers, and false prophets—with so much warfare, pestilence, hardship, and disaster, while believers are being killed and persecuted, and while false believers are defecting from their ranks, the Gospel will continue to be proclaimed. Though Satan may seem to be having his heyday, the Lord Jesus Christ will not be without a witness.

How is the Gospel preached? By both natural and supernatural means. The 144,000 who are sealed in Revelation 7 will proclaim the Gospel. Later two witnesses will be given amazing power to proclaim the Gospel and verify their authority with great signs and wonders (Rev. 11:3-6)—and ultimately they will even rise from the dead before a watching world (v. 11). And in Revelation 14, just prior to the pouring out of the bowl judgments, God sends an angel from heaven with "the everlasting gospel to preach to those who dwell on the earth—to every nation, tribe, tongue, and people—saying with a loud voice, 'Fear God and give glory to Him, for the hour of His judgment has come; and worship Him who made heaven and earth, the sea and springs of water'" (Rev. 14:6-7).

That angel is a supernatural heavenly messenger who will use some extraordinary means to broadcast the message of the Gospel to the world.

And, sadly, the result—as with all the other birth-pang signs—will simply be more judgment for those who live on earth. All but the remnant will turn a deaf ear to the message. In fact, wicked people will even step up their rebellion against God (Rev. 9:20-21).

But after the Gospel is proclaimed, the day of salvation for humanity will end (cf. 2 Cor. 6:2). *"And then the end will come"* (Matt. 24:14). God's patience finally spent, He will set His holy vengeance in full motion. The first phase of labor—"the beginning of sorrows"—is over. From here on, the world will be in its final stages before the return of Christ to establish His kingdom. But things are going to get worse before they get better.

five

THE GREAT
TRiBULATiON

$\mathcal{J}$erusalem will be a major focus of world conflict during the Tribulation. Everything Scripture says about the end times confirms this. Zechariah gave this succinct summary of the events that will occur in the Day of the Lord:

> Behold, the day of the LORD is coming, and your spoil will be divided in your midst. For I will gather all the nations to battle against Jerusalem; the city shall be taken, the houses rifled, and the women ravished. Half of the city shall go into captivity, but the remnant of the people shall not be cut off from the city. Then the LORD will go forth and fight against those nations, as He fights in the day of battle. And in that day His feet will stand on the Mount of Olives, which faces Jerusalem on the east.
>
> —14:1-4

Several other passages of Scripture also indicate that the immediate prelude to Christ's return will be the armies of the world arraying themselves for battle against Jerusalem. The apostle John's apocalyptic vision begins to reach its climax as the world's military forces gather themselves in the valley of Megiddo ("Armageddon") to go to battle against Jerusalem. All the events in the Tribulation era progress toward one great, final conflict. And in perfect harmony with the ancient prophecy of Zechariah, the apostle John foresees the return of Christ right in the midst of this cataclysmic battle (Rev. 19:11-14, 19).

JERUSALEM SURROUNDED BY ARMIES

In Luke's account of the Olivet Discourse, Jesus says, "When you see Jerusalem surrounded by armies, then know that its desolation is near" (Luke 21:20). His advice to the faithful during that time was: "Then let those who are in Judea flee to the mountains, let those who are in the midst of her depart, and let not those who are in the country enter her. For these are the days of vengeance, that all things which are written may be fulfilled" (vv. 21-22).

"Jerusalem surrounded by armies" is actually quite a familiar sight. Jerusalem was sacked by Rome in that famous and devastating siege of A.D. 70. Thousands of people did flee into the mountains, and many more traveled as refugees to various parts of the world. Josephus wrote a record of those horrible days when the armies of Titus Vespasian surrounded and attacked the city until they

> had no more people to slay or to plunder, because there remained none to be the objects of their fury, (for they would not have spared any, had there remained any other work to be done). Caesar gave orders that they should now demolish the entire city and temple, but should leave [three towers and a portion of the city wall] in order to demonstrate to posterity what kind of city it was, and how well fortified, which the Roman valor had subdued; but for all the rest of the wall, it was so thoroughly laid even with the ground by those that dug it up to the foundation, that *there was left nothing to make those that came thither believe it had ever been inhabited. (Jewish Wars,* 7:1:1, emphasis added)

Yet those were not, in the words of Luke 21:22, "the days of vengeance, [when] all things which are written may be fulfilled." Christ did not return visibly in A.D. 70. The opposing armies were not defeated by His presence. All Israel was not saved. The Jews were not grafted back into the olive tree. There is much pertaining to the Day of the Lord and His vengeance against sin that yet awaits fulfillment.

In the Middle Ages, especially during the Crusades, Jerusalem was surrounded by armies many times. Jerusalem was repeatedly attacked, and control of the city changed hands several times from the start of the First Crusade in A.D. 1095 until the time of Suleiman the Magnificent, the great Ottoman Sultan, in the early 1500s. (The stone walls and battlements encircling the Old City of Jerusalem today are actually fairly late fortifications, built in the early sixteenth century by Suleiman, a visible reminder that Jerusalem has often been "surrounded by armies.")

Even today Jerusalem is surrounded by hostile nations whose armies are in a constant state of readiness for war against Israel. After the modern state of Israel was declared in 1948, a war of independence left the city of Jerusalem divided, with Jordan retaining control over the Old City (including the temple mount and most of the historic sites). Finally, during the Six-Day War in 1967, Israeli forces captured the Old City and reunified all of Jerusalem. The city was under Jewish control for the first time in many centuries.

More than thirty years later, however, Jerusalem remains at the heart of the Israeli-Palestinian conflict, with many Arab leaders worldwide insisting that the Old City and the entire West Bank are rightfully Palestinian territory and must ultimately be ceded back as a condition of peace.

And so Jerusalem is "surrounded by armies" in a figurative sense right now, and the political situation in the Middle East is so volatile that a literal gathering of armies against Jerusalem is not at all an unlikely prospect even in our time.

So if the gathering of armies against Jerusalem is supposed to be a sign, as Luke 21:20 suggests, how can this sign be distinguished from all these other times throughout history when the city has been under siege?

Matthew's account of the Olivet Discourse answers that question.

THE ABOMINATION OF DESOLATION

According to both Matthew and Mark, Jesus described the turning point of the Tribulation in these terms: "Therefore when you see the 'abomination of desolation,' spoken of by Daniel the prophet, standing in the holy place" (whoever reads, let him understand), "then let those who are in Judea flee to the mountains" (Matt. 24:15-16).

So the definitive signal that all these things are shortly coming to pass will be the fulfillment of Daniel's prophecy about the abomination of desolation. Notice the parenthetical remark "whoever reads, let him understand." That could be something Jesus actually said as part of the Olivet Discourse (Mark includes it as well), or it could be a God-breathed editorial comment added parenthetically when the text was committed to writing by Matthew and Mark. Either way, it underscores the fact that the events Jesus outlines in this discourse belong to the prophetic future. There's an important layer of meaning beyond what is obvious: *let the reader understand.* The message clearly goes beyond the disciples themselves and speaks in a particular way to a future generation of readers who will actually see all these events unfold.

The word *abomination* speaks of something that is disgusting, repulsive, detestable, and utterly abhorrent to God. Revelation 21:27 says nothing that "causes an abomination" will be permitted to enter heaven. Throughout Scripture the term *abomination* is applied to acts of idolatry, immorality, and spiritual uncleanness. Pagan religion was particularly deemed abominable. In Revelation 17 it is applied to the consummate false religious system, represented in John's vision by a woman on whose forehead was written "MYSTERY, BABYLON THE GREAT, THE MOTHER OF HARLOTS AND OF THE ABOMINATIONS OF THE EARTH" (v. 5).

What Jesus is describing is a monstrous abomination that causes great desolation. The desolation itself is not what is intrinsically abominable, but the abomination—something like an act of gross idolatry—results in widespread devastation and ruin, most likely by launching a war.

Jesus refers to this abomination as something "spoken of by Daniel the prophet." Daniel actually mentions the abomination of desolation three times. One is in Daniel 9:27. We examined that passage and the context of Daniel's prophecy about seventy weeks in Chapter 4. But Daniel mentions and further elaborates on the abomination of desolation twice more in his prophecy, in Daniel 11:31 and 12:11. These passages shed even more light on what Jesus meant.

The whole book of Daniel is set amidst some fascinating and detailed prophecies about the rise and fall of world empires, in which Daniel (writing in the sixth century B.C.) correctly foretold the ascent and succession of several world empires, including Babylon, Persia, Greece, and Rome. This whole theme begins in Daniel 2, when Nebuchadnezzar, King of Babylon, has a mysterious dream that leaves a deep impression on his mind. But afterward he cannot remember the dream, until both the dream and its interpretation are revealed by God to Daniel. Daniel, who had been exiled in the Babylon Captivity, was serving as a counselor in Nebuchadnezzar's court.

Daniel unveils the dream, which involves a massive image with a head of gold, a chest and arms of silver, midriff and thighs of bronze, and feet made of iron and clay (vv. 31-33). His interpretation of the dream is a detailed account of world history up to and including the Roman Empire. The head of gold stands for Nebuchadnezzar (v. 38). The other segments of the image stand for successive kingdoms, representing Persia, then Greece, then Rome. The details filled in by Daniel are quite remarkable, including prophecies that were fulfilled to the letter by historical figures such as Cyrus (first king of Persia), Alexander the Great (conqueror of Persia and founder of the Macedonian Empire), Ptolemy and Seleucus (two of Alexander's generals), and the dynasties they founded—the Ptolemaic and Seleucid kings. The precise accuracy of Daniel's prophecies is one of the main reasons critics have attacked this book with such fervor, insisting that it could not really have been written by Daniel during the Jews' captivity.

Daniel 11:31 falls in the midst of a section describing a great conflict between two kings—one from the South, the other from the North (11:5-45). "The king of the South" represents the Ptolemaic dynasty (rulers of Egypt), and "the king of the North" is a reference to the Seleucid dynasty (rulers of Syria). Although the two dynasties were originally friendly, tension arose between them over control of the land of Israel, and ultimately they went to war against one another.

Daniel 11:21 describes someone who ascends to the Seleucid throne: "A vile person, to whom they will not give the honor of royalty; but he shall come in peaceably, and seize the kingdom by intrigue." Nearly all students of Scripture recognize this as a reference to the last of the major Seleucid kings, Antiochus IV.

Antiochus came to the throne when his brother, Seleucus IV, was poisoned by a corrupt tax collector named Heliodorus, who hoped to gain the throne for himself. The rightful heir to the throne was Demetrius, son of Seleucus IV, but conspirators loyal to Heliodorus were holding Demetrius hostage in Rome. Antiochus IV, taking advantage of the circumstances, expelled Heliodorus and claimed the throne for himself. Just as Daniel's prophecy had indicated, he seized the throne by intrigue but without war, even though he was not really entitled to it.

Antiochus bestowed on himself the title "Epiphanes," meaning "manifest one" or "splendid one." It was for all practical purposes a claim of deity for himself. But his enemies, varying the word slightly, nicknamed him "Epimanes," meaning "madman."

Pretending to be the defender of Jerusalem, Antiochus went to war against Egypt, then used spoils plundered from Egypt to win support from influential people in Israel. This seems to be precisely what Daniel prophesied in 11:24: "He shall enter peaceably, even into the richest places of the province; and he shall do what his fathers have not done, nor his forefathers: he shall disperse among them the plunder, spoil, and riches; and he shall devise his plans against the strongholds, but only for a time."

History records that as he prepared to launch a final assault against Egypt in 168 B.C., he received orders from Rome via Cyprus (where the Roman fleet was anchored at the time) that he was not to make war against the Ptolemies. Antiochus, humiliated but unwilling to go against both Rome and Egypt, reluctantly withdrew from Egypt, and on his way back to Syria he decided to vent his rage against Jerusalem. That is precisely what Daniel had foretold more than three centuries before: "Ships from Cyprus shall come against him; therefore he shall be grieved, and return in rage against the holy covenant, and do damage" (11:30).

Two Apocryphal books, 1 and 2 Maccabees, record Antiochus' treachery. He entered Jerusalem under the pretense of peace. He then waited until the Sabbath and ordered his army of more than 250,000 to carry out wholesale slaughter against the Jews. They met with very little resistance because of the Jews' rigid observance of the Sabbath laws (2 Maccabees 5:24-26). Antiochus then deliberately set several Jewish apostates (enemies of Israel's covenant with Jehovah) in power over the occupied city, again fulfilling Daniel's prophecy to the letter: "So he shall return and show regard for those who forsake the holy covenant" (Dan. 11:30). He set out deliberately to defile the temple, and this he did by sacrificing a pig (an unclean and forbidden animal, according to Lev. 11:7) on the altar and forcing the priests to eat its flesh.

His design, moreover, was to set up a new religion of his own, a thoroughly pagan kind of worship that was a mockery of Judaism.

> King Antiochus wrote to his whole kingdom, that all should be one people, and every one should leave his laws: so all the heathen agreed according to the commandment of the king. Yea, many also of the Israelites consented to his religion, and sacrificed unto idols, and profaned the sabbath. For the king had sent letters by messengers unto Jerusalem and the cities of Judah that they should follow the strange laws of the land, and forbid burnt offerings, and sacrifice, and drink offerings, in the temple; and that they should profane the sabbaths and festival days: and pollute the sanctuary and holy people: set up altars, and groves, and chapels of idols, and sacrifice swine's flesh, and unclean beasts: that they should also leave their chil-

dren uncircumcised, and make their souls abominable with all manner of uncleanness and profanation: to the end they might forget the law, and change all the ordinances, and whosoever would not do according to the commandment of the king, he said, he should die. (1 Maccabees 1:41-50)

In other words, it was forbidden for anyone to observe the Old Testament dietary laws, the Sabbath laws, circumcision, or anything else distinctly Jewish. Notice that Antiochus' stated goal was "that all should be one people." In other words, he wanted to establish a new one-world religion, beginning at Jerusalem. Under the pretense of "unity," this megalomaniacal madman sought to found a religion that was an amalgam of many religions, but in which he was the ultimate object of worship. And there is little doubt that his real goal was eventually to conquer the whole world and impose his religion everywhere.

It was at this time that Antiochus committed the act usually associated with the abomination of desolation: "Now the fifteenth day of the month Chislev, in the hundred forty and fifth year, they set up the abomination of desolation upon the altar" (1 Maccabees 1:54). History records that this was an image of Zeus and an altar to Zeus, built right on the Jews' altar of the burnt offering. This put an end to the daily sacrifices to Jehovah in the temple.

Again history accords precisely with Daniel's prophecy: "Forces shall be mustered by him, and they shall defile the sanctuary fortress; then they shall take away the daily sacrifices, and place there the abomination of desolation" (Dan. 11:31).

Daniel mentions the abomination of desolation only one more time, and that comes at the end of his prophecy. He recounts how he heard things he did not understand. "Then I said, 'My lord, what shall be the end of these things?' And he said, 'Go your way, Daniel, for the words are closed up and sealed till the time of the end'" (12:8-9). This clearly signifies that elements of Daniel's prophecy had implications beyond the Maccabean era, applying to "the time of the end." Daniel then adds this final prophecy from the Lord Himself:

"Many shall be purified, made white, and refined, but the wicked shall do wickedly; and none of the wicked shall understand, but the wise shall understand. And from the time that the daily sacrifice is taken away, and the abomination of desolation is set up, there shall be one thousand two hundred and ninety days. Blessed is he who waits, and comes to the one thousand three hundred and thirty-five days. But you, go your way till the end; for you shall rest, and will arise to your inheritance at the end of the days."

—12:10-13

The "many" who "shall be purified, made white, and refined" seem to be those who will be redeemed in the final salvation of Israel. Counting from the abomination of desolation, 1,290 days were to elapse. But Daniel's prophecy does not expressly state what happens next. The time span closely corresponds to the 1,260 days mentioned in Revelation 11:3, which is precisely three and a half years (counting years of 360 days, in accord with the Jewish calendar). As we noted in the previous chapter, many passages refer to an end-time period of three and a half years, including Revelation 11:2 ("forty-two months") and Daniel 12:7 ("a time, times, and half a time"). All those references are clearly intertwined and refer to the same period of time, the second half of the Tribulation, culminating in the triumphant return of Christ.

But the 1,290 days of Daniel 12:11 include an additional thirty days, and the 1,335 days of verse 12 include another forty-five days on top of that. Why? Revelation 20 indicates that Christ will establish His earthly kingdom for a thousand years, soon after His return in glory. The extra seventy-five days may merely reflect the time that elapses between the state of war in which Israel is "completely shattered" (Dan. 12:7) and the institution of Messiah's kingdom from a rebuilt Jerusalem. Some of those extra days could also represent the time it will take for the judgment of the nations and the final restoration of Israel to take place in the wake of Christ's return.

In any case, since Christ Himself quite plainly stated that the "abomination of desolation" was a yet-future reality, we must conclude that the ultimate eschatalogical meaning of Daniel's prophecy was not fulfilled but merely foreshadowed in the events of Antiochus IV's time. The great and final abomination of desolation awaits future fulfillment in the middle of Daniel's seventieth week, during the Tribulation era. The Antichrist, following the same pattern as Antiochus Epiphanes, will evidently pretend peace with Israel. Although Scripture does not expressly identify the nature of the "covenant" he confirms (cf. Dan. 9:27), some have speculated that the Antichrist will work out a peace treaty that gives Israel the right to rebuild a temple on Mount Moriah. That could well be the case, since the temple figures so large in all these prophecies.

In the middle of the week, the Antichrist will commit an act of abomination, probably by defiling the rebuilt temple with an idol of himself. That scenario is suggested by the account of the Beast who appears in Revelation 13. The apostle John records that in his vision the False Prophet "was granted power to give breath to the image of the beast, that the image of the beast should both speak and cause as many as would not worship the image of the beast to be killed" (Rev. 13:15). The apostle Paul describes a similar scene, when "the man of sin is revealed, the son of perdition, who opposes and exalts himself above all that is called God or that is worshiped, so that he sits as God in the temple of God, showing himself that he is God" (2 Thess. 2:3-4). Antichrist will thus turn against Israel, set himself up as God, and demand an end to all other forms of worship. The resemblance of this to Daniel's abomination of desolation and the history of Antiochus is impossible to miss.

Whatever the abomination of desolation is, when the time comes and the event actually occurs, it should be fairly obvious to all believers who are familiar with Scripture. That's why Matthew 24:15 says, "Whoever reads, let him understand." This will be the single most important sign that the Tribulation has given way to the *Great* Tribulation and that three and a half years of sheer affliction and hardship will descend on the world.

PERIL AND CALAMITY

When the abomination of desolation appears, it will signal the onset of many grave dangers, not only for the remnant of believers, who will face a worsening of the already-severe persecutions, but more particularly for the rest of the world, which will be on the brink of the judgment of God. So Jesus says:

> *"Let those who are in Judea flee to the mountains. Let him who is on the housetop not go down to take anything out of his house. And let him who is in the field not go back to get his clothes. But woe to those who are pregnant and to those who are nursing babies in those days! And pray that your flight may not be in winter or on the Sabbath. For then there will be great tribulation, such as has not been since the beginning of the world until this time, no, nor ever shall be. And unless those days were shortened, no flesh would be saved; but for the elect's sake those days will be shortened."*
>
> —MATT. 24:16-22

All the birth-pang signs at that time will increase dramatically in their intensity and frequency. The difference between the Tribulation and the Great Tribulation is comparable to the difference between labor and hard labor.

Apparently the Beast will not only defile the Jewish temple, but he may also make it the permanent throne from which he rules. Paul writes in 2 Thessalonians 2:4: "He sits as God in the temple of God, showing himself that he is God." It is not necessary to rule out a future literal fulfillment of that prophecy, especially if it refers to a rebuilt temple.

One more fact confirms that these things will occur in Jerusalem in a rebuilt temple. Jesus says when the abomination of desolation occurs, the danger will be especially great for those living in and around Judea. He commands them to flee into the mountains. During the siege of Jerusalem by Rome in A.D. 70, many Jews literally did hide in the mountains and the wilderness areas near Jerusalem. The famous twenty-acre fortress at Masada (built in the first century B.C. by Herod the Great as an emergency refuge for him and his family) was used as a hiding-place for a large community of Jews who fled the Roman armies in A.D. 66. After seven years of unsuccessfully assaulting that fortress, Rome's tenth legion finally completed an immense rock-and-gravel siege ramp on the western side of Masada. When troops finally broke over the top, what they found was chilling. About a thousand Jewish zealots had committed mass suicide rather than submit to capture and abuse from the Romans. The events of the Tribulation will feature horrors like this, but on a much greater scale.

Another reason Christ's warning is particularly germane to "those who are in Judea" is that the atrocities of those days will specifically target the Jews. Zechariah 13:8-9, describing events just prior to Christ's return (14:4), suggests that a campaign of genocide will be waged against the Jewish people:

> *"And it shall come to pass in all the land," says the LORD, "that two-thirds in it shall be cut off and die, but one-third shall be left in it: I will bring the one-third through the fire, will refine them as silver is refined, and test them as gold is tested. They will call on My name, and I will answer them. I will say, 'This is My people'; and each one will say, 'The LORD is my God.'"*

As many as two-thirds will die, and the rest—the remnant who will ultimately be saved—will call on the Lord. Many who die will be people who came to faith in Christ during the early part of the Tribulation. Revelation 7:14 describes a large crowd of white-robed worshipers in heaven as "the ones who come out of the great tribulation." The apostle John also refers to the Beast's campaign of terror as "war with the saints" (13:7), and he portrays the Beast's false religious system as a woman who is "drunk with the blood of the saints and with the blood of the martyrs of Jesus" (17:6).

Those who are not killed will be given refuge in the mountains by God Himself. Revelation 12 likens Israel to a woman ("the woman who gave birth to the male Child [Christ]," v. 13). John recounts how in his vision, "The woman was given two wings of a great eagle, that she might fly into the wilderness to her place, where she is nourished for a time and times and half a time, from the presence of the serpent" (v. 14). The language is clearly symbolic; eagle's wings may signify some kind of angelic assistance or custody for those who flee.

The urgency of the situation is clear from our Lord's words in Matthew 24. People should not even take time to gather up their personal effects. Houses in Jesus' day had stairways outside leading to the roof, where the family relaxed in the cool of the evening. Jesus says those who happen to be on the roof when they hear about the abomination of desolation should not even go back into the house to get any personal possessions before fleeing to the mountains (v. 17). The farmer working in his field should not even return to the other side of the field to collect his jacket (v. 18). No material possession is worth the risk of even the slightest delay. Time is of the essence.

These are unique words in all the teaching of Christ. Everywhere else He urges His followers to take up their cross and follow Him, to be bold in their testimony, and to take a stand for Him even amid the worst kinds of hostility. But the abomination of desolation will change all that. It will virtually signal the end of Christ's testimony to the world and the beginning of His judgment against His enemies. Once it occurs, He will no longer command His people to go into all the world with the Gospel, but instead will urge them to flee to the mountains for their own safety.

Why does our Lord single out pregnant and nursing mothers for a special warning (v. 19)? Not only is it more difficult for them to flee, but if they are caught, the consequences would surely be worse for them. Hosea 13:16 predicted a time when the inhabitants of Samaria (the district immediately north of Judea) would "fall by the sword, their infants shall be dashed in pieces, and their women with child ripped open."

The situation will be so horrific that when the abomination of desolation occurs, the people of God should flee without the slightest hesitation. Delay will be costly. Every second counts. And Jesus said to pray that it doesn't happen in inclement weather or on the Sabbath (v. 20). He was *not* suggesting that it would be a sinful violation of the Sabbath to flee for one's life (cf. Luke 6:9). But legalistic Sabbatarians might try to impede or stone people whom they believed were guilty of profaning the Sabbath, just as they had done with Jesus (cf. John 7:19-23).

Christ thus paints the picture in the darkest tones possible. It will be a time of "great tribulation, such as has not been since the beginning of the world until this time, no, nor ever shall be" (v. 21). All the world's holocausts and disasters combined could never compare with this. Though many horrible pogroms and slaughters have been brought against the Jews over the centuries, none of them precisely fits the description Jesus gives here. This clearly speaks of a time yet to come.

And unless those days are "shortened," Jesus says (v. 22), no life on earth will be saved. The days *will* be shortened for the elect's sake, He promises, employing a Greek expression that can mean "cut short," in the sense of stopping instantly. He might therefore be promising that the days of the Great Tribulation will be suddenly brought to a screeching halt, as opposed to winding down slowly at the end. Another possibility is that He means the daylight hours will be supernaturally cut short, so that the darkening of the sun and moon spoken of in verse 29 would have the merciful effect of diminishing the torment of those days and making it easier for the people of God to hide from their oppressors. Christ does not suggest, however, that the time of the Great Tribulation will be "shortened" to something less than three and a half years. Since the precise length of this era is repeatedly given in Scripture, the truthfulness of God's Word would seem to demand that the full measure of that time be played out.

VULTURES GATHERING TOGETHER

Again Christ raises the issue of false messiahs: "Then if anyone says to you, 'Look, here is the Christ!' or 'There!' do not believe it. For false christs and false prophets will rise and show great signs and wonders to deceive, if possible, even the elect. See, I have told you beforehand" (vv. 23-25). The birth-pang signs are still coming in ever harder waves.

And now the false messiahs will even have the power to work great signs and wonders. These "miracles" will be so convincing that even the elect are liable to be misled, except for one thing—God sovereignly enables Christ's sheep to hear His voice and to distinguish it from the voices of hirelings and thieves. "They will by no means follow a stranger, but will flee from him, for they do not know the voice of strangers" (John 10:5).

Our Lord's warning seems to suggest that false messiahs will actually infiltrate the ranks of those who flee. Though the people of God can take flight from Antichrist's persecutions, they will not be able to escape Satan's lying minions, who will evidently follow them into hiding. Even in their exile from the threat of annihilation, the refugees will constantly hear lying people claim, "Look, here is the Christ!"; "There!" (v. 23). "Look, He is in the desert!" Or, "He is in the inner rooms!" All such claims will be lies, perhaps even deliberately designed to lure the refugees out of hiding. Believers are solemnly instructed in advance to pay no attention to them.

So how will anyone know when the true Christ finally appears? How can the true Christ be distinguished from all counterfeits? It will be obvious to all: "For as the lightning comes from the east and flashes to the west, so also will the coming of the Son of Man be" (v. 27). "Behold, He is coming with clouds, and every eye will see Him" (Rev. 1:7). His coming will be no secret. Suddenly, publicly, and gloriously He will return, and His coming will be universally visible! Not only will those in hiding from persecution recognize Him, but so will His enemies. He "comes with ten thousands of His saints, to execute judgment on all, to convict all who are ungodly among them of all their ungodly deeds which they have committed in an ungodly way, and of all the harsh things which ungodly sinners have spoken against Him" (Jude 14-15).

And when Christ appears, His people and His enemies will

exchange places, as it were. Those who have been in hiding in the mountains and caves will be set free from all fear and danger, while their tormentors will seek refuge from the righteous wrath of God, pleading for the rocks and mountains to fall on them and hide them from the wrath of the Lamb (cf. Rev. 6:16-17).

To underscore how obvious His return will be, our Lord employs what may have been a familiar aphorism: "For wherever the carcass is, there the eagles will be gathered together" (v. 28). When a animal lies dead or rotting in the desert, its location can be pinpointed with accuracy for miles because of the buzzards circling overhead. Christ is saying that in a similar way, His return will be obvious to everyone near and far.

By the end of the Great Tribulation, the wretchedness and spiritual decay of this world will make it a lifeless carcass. Christ will then appear to dispose of it in final judgment. So the imagery of carrion birds is a figure of judgment, underscoring what is taught everywhere in Scripture about the glorious appearing of Christ: It will be accompanied by dreadful judgments against his enemies. The apostle Paul says he will return "in flaming fire taking vengeance on those who do not know God" (2 Thess. 1:8). Revelation 19:11-16 pictures Christ coming out of heaven on a white horse, accompanied by the saints and angels in all the glory of heaven. He comes with a sword in His hand, wearing a blood-spattered garment, bringing judgment on the world and destroying all the armies who array themselves in battle against Him.

Thus the stage is set for the Second Coming. The world has utterly spent God's mercy and patience. His people have waited long enough. "Now when these things begin to happen, look up and lift up your heads, because your redemption draws near" (Luke 21:28).

Six

Signs in the Sky

A few years ago I taught a series on the doctrine of the church in a marathon-like, week-long series of all-day sessions in a conference for pastors in Kazakhstan. By Thursday morning we were deep into the pastoral epistles. During the morning break that day, one of the men who had helped organize the conference came to me and said, "Some of the pastors are asking when you're going to get to the *good* part."

"What's 'the good part'?" I asked.

"Why, it's the future of the church, the part where Jesus returns," he answered, utterly surprised that I did not instantly know what "the good part" is. "They're eager to hear about the return of Christ."

I certainly understand the desire to jump to "the good part." It's the same feeling I get whenever I study the Olivet Discourse. I suppose as the disciples sat on the Mount of Olives listening to Christ paint the bleak-sounding scenario of end-time events, they must have also been longing for Him to jump to "the good part."

So far the entire discourse has been filled with prophecies of doom and gloom. Christ started by predicting a long list of birth pangs. Those were bad enough, but things grew even worse after the abomination of desolation. And even now, as His prophetic account approaches the climax of the Great Tribulation, the world has yet to experience even more darkness before the visible dawning of Christ's glory.

The Last Great Cosmic Signs

At the end of the previous chapter, we saw that Christ promised that His coming would be obvious to all: "As the lightning comes from the east and flashes to the west, so also will the coming of the Son of Man be" (Matt. 24:27). One of the factors ensuring that no one misses Christ's return is the cosmic nature of the final signs: "Immediately after the tribulation of those days the sun will be darkened, and the moon will not give its light; the stars will fall from heaven, and the powers of the heavens will be shaken" (v. 29). Luke's parallel account adds some grim details: "There will be signs in the sun, in the moon, and in the stars; and on the earth distress of nations, with perplexity, the sea and the waves roaring; men's hearts failing them from fear and the expectation of those things which are coming on the earth, for the powers of heaven will be shaken" (Luke 21:25-26).[1]

Such signs will have a sensational worldwide effect. Every person in every nation of the world will take note. Luke says some will even experience heart failure because of the sheer terror of these phenomena. The whole world's attention will immediately be drawn heavenward. The sense of dread and worldwide panic is scarcely imaginable. Finally, out of that same disquieted sky, Christ will reappear in all His glory.

Notice carefully how Christ leads up to this final great turning-point in His discourse.

The sequence of events. Our Lord speaks expressly about the timing of these signs. He says the cosmic signs will occur at the very end of the Great Tribulation: "*Immediately* after the tribulation of those days" (v. 29, emphasis added). These great signs in the sky seem to be to the second half of the Tribulation what the abomination of desolation was to the first—a clear and unmistakable signal that the era has reached an end and something significant is about to occur.

"The tribulation of those days" in this context can only refer to the era Jesus has just been describing—and in particular, the time of the Great Tribulation launched by the abomination of desolation. Notice that these cosmic signs occur *immediately* after the Tribulation. Here is another powerful reason to reject the preterist interpretation of the Olivet Discourse: No great cosmic signs like this ever occurred in connection with the destruction of Jerusalem in A.D. 70.

Many preterists, undeterred by this, simply dismiss Jesus' language as metaphorical. They claim He is speaking symbolically about the collapse of the Old-Covenant era, not literally predicting vast signs in the sun and moon. For example, preterist Gary Demar writes:

> The darkening of the sun and moon and the falling of the stars, coupled with the shaking of the heavens (24:29), are more descriptive ways of saying that "heaven and earth will pass away" (24:35). In other contexts, when stars fall, they fall to the earth, a sure sign of temporal judgment (Isaiah 14:12; Daniel 8:10; Revelation 6:13; 9:1; 12:4). So then, the "passing away of heaven and earth" is the passing away of the old covenant world of Judaism (1 Corinthians 2:8).[2]

In other words, Demar believes that when Jesus says, "Heaven and earth will pass away" (v. 35), He is not speaking of any literal eschatalogical cosmic judgment that will really destroy the earth. Instead, the passing away of heaven and earth, according to Demar, is merely metaphorical language that speaks of the transition from Old Covenant to New. Similarly, Demar claims, the darkening of the sun and moon in Matthew 24:29 are merely metaphorical terms that refer to the passing away of the Jewish dispensation.

Demar and other preterists impose a similar interpretive grid on most of the Olivet Discourse, employing allegory and symbolic language to make as many of the prophecies as possible fit the events of A.D. 70. In so doing, they utterly divest much of the discourse of any real significance, turning great cosmic signs into mere metaphors about the transition between covenants.

Most preterists stop short of allegorizing away the bodily return of Christ (the error of *hyper*-preterism).[3] But it is frankly hard to see how any preterist could ever give a credible refutation of hyper-preterism from Scripture, given the fact that the hermeneutical approach underlying both views is identical.[4] Hyper-preterists simply apply the preterist method more consistently to *all* New Testament prophecy. They start with the remainder of the Olivet Discourse, spiritualizing away not only the cosmic signs, but also the literal bodily return of Christ. Further imposing their interpretive grid on all of Scripture, most modern hyper-preterists ultimately defuse *every* biblical reference to yet-future events.

The typical preterist will claim that the apocalyptic language Christ employs in this passage gives sufficient warrant for interpreting the cosmic signs allegorically, symbolically, and spiritually. After all, they protest, imposing a strict literalism on all such passages throughout Scripture would have the moon literally turning to blood (Joel 2:31) and the stars literally falling from the sky to the earth (Rev. 9:1).

It is certainly true that the apocalyptic sections of Scripture are often filled with symbolic language. In Revelation 17:3, for example, the apostle John describes a woman riding a seven-headed beast. He later explains that "The seven heads are seven mountains on which the woman sits" (Rev. 17:9), forcing us to conclude that the "woman" is not a literal woman but a symbolic figure who represents either the city of Rome (well-known for being situated on seven hills) or, as John himself goes on to imply, the evil system behind seven successive world empires (v. 10). Symbolic language like that is sometimes clearly explained, sometimes not. But the context always makes clear when symbolism is being employed.

Most would agree there is a degree of symbolism in Matthew 24:29. Almost no one expects the stars to fall to earth literally. It's possible, too, that the sun might not be extinguished literally; rather, the sun's light could simply be partly or totally obscured from the earth (cf. Ezek. 32:7). So I agree that *wooden* literalism is not necessary to get the right sense of Jesus' words.

But even granting a reasonable degree of obvious symbolism, the plain sense of these words still does not allow the preterist interpretation. Christ is predicting cosmic signs of some kind—signs so spectacular that no one on earth can possibly miss them. His whole point in this context is to reassure His people that when He returns, it will be spectacularly obvious to one and all. There will be no possibility of confusion about whether He has truly returned or not.

But the preterist interpretation utterly empties Jesus' words of that reassurance. If the preterists are right, not only did the whole world completely miss Christ's return on the clouds in glory, but so did virtually everyone in the church. Because with relatively few exceptions, practically every believer in 2,000 years of Christendom has believed Matthew 24:30 speaks of an event yet to happen.

The oldest extra-biblical Christian document known to exist is *The Didache*, which is a simple distillation of Bible doctrine from the early church. Most scholars believe it was written near the close of the first century, most likely after A.D. 80. It was certainly used and cited in the early centuries by many Church Fathers (as well as by the historian Eusebius).[5] So its early existence is well documented. The full text of *The Didache* was rediscovered little more than a hundred years ago, in a codex found in Constantinople in 1873. This document proves that those who actually lived through the events of A.D. 70 regarded Matthew 24:29-31—and the entire Olivet Discourse—as yet-unfulfilled prophecy.

> For in the last days the false prophets and corrupters shall be multiplied, and the sheep shall be turned into wolves, and love shall be turned into hate. For as lawlessness increaseth, they shall hate one another and shall persecute and betray. And then the world-deceiver shall appear as a son of God; and shall work signs and wonders, and the earth shall be delivered into his hands; and he shall do unholy things, which have never been since the world began. Then all created mankind shall come to the fire of testing, and many shall be offended and perish; but they that endure in their faith shall be saved by the Curse Himself. And then shall the signs of the truth appear; first a sign of a rift in the heaven, then a sign of a voice of a trumpet, and thirdly a resurrection of the dead; yet not of all, but as it was said the Lord shall come and all His saints with

Him. Then shall the world see the Lord coming upon the clouds of heaven. (*Didache* 16:3-8)

Justin Martyr was probably born in the first century and certainly knew many believers who had lived through the events of A.D. 70. He also clearly regarded the Second Coming of Christ as a yet-future event. In his *Dialogue with Trypho,* Justin writes:

> Two advents of Christ have been announced: the one, in which He is set forth as suffering, inglorious, dishonoured, and crucified; but the other, in which He shall come from heaven with glory, when the man of apostasy, who speaks strange things against the Most High, shall venture to do unlawful deeds on the earth against us the Christians. . . . The rest of the prophecy shall be fulfilled at His second coming. (chap. 110)

So Justin, who could not have written much more than fifty years after the destruction of Jerusalem, still saw a future fulfillment of both the Tribulation prophecies and the return of Christ in glory.

That means if modern preterists are correct, some of the most astute students of Scripture and leaders in the early church utterly missed the fulfillment of the very prophecy Jesus indicated no one in the world would possibly be able to miss![6]

But it twists Jesus' words to turn them into mere allegory. What He was describing was an event long foretold in Scripture, an event so monumental that it would be a signal to the whole world. Moreover, Christ's coming was to usher in the final salvation of Israel, not the end of national Israel as the people of God.

The scene in the heavens. The cosmic signs Jesus gave in His discourse would have been thoroughly familiar to any student of Old Testament Messianic prophecy. These very same signs involving the sun, moon, and stars were well-known harbingers of the Messianic deliverance everyone in Israel looked for. The same signs were also heralds of the retribution he would mete out to His enemies. These were the emblems of the Day of the Lord.

> *Behold, the day of the LORD comes, cruel with both wrath and fierce anger, to lay the land desolate: and He will destroy its sinners from it. For* the stars of heaven and their constellations will not give their light: the sun shall be darkened in his going forth, and the moon will not cause its light to shine. *I will punish the world for their evil, and the wicked for their iniquity; I will halt the arrogance of the proud, and will lay low the haughtiness of the terrible. I will make a man more rare than fine gold; a man more than the golden wedge of Ophir. Therefore I will shake the heavens, and the earth will move out of her place, in the wrath of the LORD of hosts, and in the day of His fierce anger. It shall be as the hunted gazelle, and as a sheep that no man takes up. Every man will turn to his own people, and everyone will flee to his own land. Everyone who is found will be thrust through, and everyone who is captured will fall by the sword.*
> —ISA. 13:9-15, EMPHASIS ADDED[7]

Later, describing the same scene of worldwide judgment, Isaiah wrote:

> *Come near, you nations, to hear; and heed, you people! Let the earth hear, and all that is in it, the world and all things that come forth from it. For the indignation of the LORD is against all nations, and His fury against all their armies; He has utterly destroyed them, He has given them over to the slaughter. Also their slain shall be thrown out; their stench shall rise from their corpses, and the mountains shall be melted with their blood.* All the host of heaven shall be dissolved, and the heavens shall be rolled up like a scroll; all their host shall fall down as the leaf falls from the vine, and as fruit falling from a fig tree. *For My sword shall be bathed in heaven; indeed it shall come down on Edom, and on the people of My curse, for judgment.*
> —ISA. 34:1-5, EMPHASIS ADDED

The immediate context of Isaiah 34 describes the coming King of Israel reigning in His glory, building in Jerusalem "a tabernacle that will not be taken down," and making that city "a quiet home" (33:20)—a clear description of the millennial kingdom. The rest of Isaiah 34 describes the systematic judgment of all the nations. Then chapter 35 returns to the description of the earthly kingdom, in which "the desert shall rejoice and blossom as the rose" (35:1). "And the ransomed of the LORD shall return, and come to Zion with singing, with everlasting joy on their heads" (v. 10).

Joel foretold the same cosmic signs. "And I will show wonders in the heavens and in the earth: Blood and fire and pillars of smoke. The sun shall be turned into darkness, and the moon into blood, before the coming of the great and awesome day of the LORD" (Joel 2:30-31).[8] "The sun and moon will grow dark, and the stars will diminish their brightness" (3:15). Those words are set in the midst of millennial and end-times prophecies too. Joel 2:32 goes on to prophesy about the salvation of the Jewish remnant: "In Mount Zion and in Jerusalem there shall be deliverance, as the Lord has said, among the remnant whom the LORD calls." Joel 3 is filled with similar references: "For behold, in those days and at that time, when I bring back the captives of Judah and Jerusalem, I will also gather all nations, and bring them down to the Valley of Jehoshaphat; and I will enter into judgment with them there" (vv. 1-2). Both the salvation of Israel and the judgment of the nations are constant themes wherever the cosmic-sign prophecies are found in Scripture.

The disciples' thoughts, when they heard mention of the cosmic signs, would have gone immediately to the Old Testament prophecies about the Day of the Lord. They knew Scripture had long foretold a time when God would shake the heavens, just as Jesus was prophesying here (cf. Isa. 13:13; Joel 3:16). And they knew such signs were associated with the Day of the Lord.

What did Jesus mean when He said "the powers of the heavens will be shaken" (Matt. 24:29)? He made no explanation. But remember that He is the One who "uphold[s] all things by the word of His power" (Heb. 1:3). He could merely speak the word, and gravity would weaken, the orbits of the planets would fluctuate, the very stars would appear to fall. None of that is beyond His power. In fact, if He but withdrew a fraction of His sustaining power, the entire universe would cease to function normally. The heavens and all the forces of energy would become unstable. Who knows what all the shaking of the heavens might entail? But one thing is certain: it will be terrifying when it happens.

Haggai wrote, "For thus says the LORD of hosts: 'Once more (it is a little while) I will shake heaven and earth, the sea and dry land; and I will shake all nations, and they shall come to the Desire of All Nations, and I will fill this temple with glory,' says the LORD of hosts" (2:6-7). There again, the Old Testament prophets connected these cosmic signs, including the shaking of the heavens, with the coming of the Messiah to judge the earth and establish His kingdom.

The sign in the sky. At that point there will be one remaining sign to come. It is the glorious appearing of Christ Himself. Here we finally reach "the good part": "Then the sign of the Son of Man will appear in heaven, and then all the tribes of the earth will mourn, and they will see the Son of Man coming on the clouds of heaven with power and great glory" (Matt. 24:30). Believers have long hoped for this moment (Titus 2:13).

This whole discourse had begun when the disciples asked Christ to tell them "the sign of [His] coming, and of the end of the age" (v. 3). This is that sign. His coming *is* what signifies the end of the age. It is the sign of signs—the glorious appearing of the Son of Man Himself.

Notice that Christ reiterates that His appearing will be universally visible. Every tribe on earth will see Him coming on the clouds of heaven. Bible students have long pondered how this will be possible. Some of the Church Fathers speculated that the whole world would see an enormous blazing cross in the darkened sky. They had no earthly idea how a single event could be witnessed by everyone on the globe at once. More recent students of prophecy have less to grapple with in that question, since His coming could easily be made visible worldwide via television.

Whatever the explanation, note that it is not a blazing cross or the *shekinah* glory or any other symbol of Christ's presence that appears in heaven; it is Christ Himself. *He* is the sign of signs. When the sun and moon are darkened, when the world's fear and hatred of God are elevated to unprecedented heights, suddenly Christ Himself will pierce through all that darkness and sin and return to win His final triumph.

He comes "on the clouds of heaven" (v. 30). When He ascended from earth into heaven, Scripture says, "A cloud received Him out of their sight" (Acts 1:9). An angel then appeared and told the disciples, "This same Jesus, who was taken up from you into heaven, will so come in like manner as you saw Him go into heaven" (v. 11). So it is fitting that He will return with clouds.

Revelation 1:7 perfectly echoes Jesus' words about His coming: "Behold, He is coming with clouds, and every eye will see Him, even they who pierced Him. And all the tribes of the earth will mourn because of Him." Earth's tribes will "mourn" His coming chiefly because they will know that He brings judgment for them, and that judgment is just.

Moreover, He comes "with power and great glory" (Matt. 24:30). That is surely something of an understatement. His return will be the greatest display of power the earth has ever witnessed. Zechariah 14:3-4 describes it in these terms:

> *Then the LORD will go forth and fight against those nations, as He fights in the day of battle. And in that day His feet will stand on the Mount of Olives, which faces Jerusalem on the east. And the Mount of Olives shall be split in two, from east to west, making a very large valley; half of the mountain shall move toward the north and half of it toward the south.*

Revelation 19 pictures the grand scene:

> *I saw heaven opened, and behold, a white horse. And He who sat on him was called Faithful and True, and in righteousness He judges*

and makes war. His eyes were like a flame of fire, and on His head were many crowns. He had a name written that no one knew except Himself. He was clothed with a robe dipped in blood, and His name is called The Word of God. And the armies in heaven, clothed in fine linen, white and clean, followed Him on white horses. Now out of His mouth goes a sharp sword, that with it He should strike the nations. And He Himself will rule them with a rod of iron. He Himself treads the winepress of the fierceness and wrath of Almighty God. And He has on His robe and on His thigh a name written: KING OF KINGS AND LORD OF LORDS.

Then I saw an angel standing in the sun; and he cried with a loud voice, saying to all the birds that fly in the midst of heaven, "Come and gather together for the supper of the great God, that you may eat the flesh of kings, the flesh of captains, the flesh of mighty men, the flesh of horses and of those who sit on them, and the flesh of all people, free and slave, both small and great." And I saw the beast, the kings of the earth, and their armies, gathered together to make war against Him who sat on the horse and against His army. Then the beast was captured, and with him the false prophet who worked signs in his presence, by which he deceived those who received the mark of the beast and those who worshiped his image. These two were cast alive into the lake of fire burning with brimstone. And the rest were killed with the sword which proceeded from the mouth of Him who sat on the horse. And all the birds were filled with their flesh.

—VV. 11-21

The armies accompanying Christ in heaven will doubtless include both the redeemed who were caught up alive, as well as those who were raised from the grave, at the Rapture. When Paul speaks of the Rapture, he promises that all those who are caught up "shall always be with the Lord" (1 Thess. 4:17). Many passages of Scripture promise that when He returns, He will bring us with Him: "When Christ who is our life appears, then you also will appear with Him in glory" (Col. 3:4). "The LORD my God will come, and all the saints with You" (Zech. 14:5). "Behold, the Lord comes with ten thousands of His saints" (Jude 14).

And notice that He immediately executes vengeance on the Antichrist and the evil hordes of earth. As for the Antichrist, the lawless one, "The Lord will consume [him] with the breath of His mouth and destroy [him] with the brightness of His coming" (2 Thess. 2:8). The rest of the wicked are destroyed with the sword that proceeds from Christ's mouth (Rev. 19:21), possibly signifying that He judges and slays them merely by speaking the Word of God. Both the Beast and the False Prophet are cast alive into the lake of fire (v. 20). The rest of the dead are kept in the grave throughout the millennial kingdom, then resurrected for judgment and cast into eternal perdition (20:5, 14-15).

THE GATHERING OF THE ELECT

Christ has more work than judgment to do at His appearing. This is not only a day of judgment; it is that glorious day when "all Israel will be saved, as it is written: 'The Deliverer will come out of Zion, and He will turn away ungodliness from Jacob'" (Rom. 11:26). The elect will be gathered by the angels "from the four winds, from one end of heaven to the other" and brought before Christ (Matt. 24:31). For the wicked of the earth, Christ's coming will mean final judgment. For the elect, it will be the consummation of their redemption.

Zechariah had prophesied this day of judgment for the world and redemption for Israel long ago:

> "It shall be in that day that I will seek to destroy all the nations that come against Jerusalem. And I will pour on the house of David and on the inhabitants of Jerusalem the Spirit of grace and supplication; then they will look on Me whom they pierced. Yes, they will mourn for Him as one mourns for his only son, and grieve for Him as one grieves for a firstborn. In that day there shall be a great mourning in Jerusalem, like the mourning at Hadad Rimmon in the plain of Megiddo."
>
> —12:9-11

Seeing with their own eyes the One whom Israel rejected and pierced, now fully realizing that He was the promised Messiah all along, the remnant will mourn. But it will be a short-lived mourning, for the Lord Himself will turn it into a day of joy: "In that day a fountain shall be opened for the house of David and for the inhabitants of Jerusalem, for sin and for uncleanness" (13:1).

> *And in that day it shall be that living waters shall flow from Jerusalem, half of them toward the eastern sea and half of them toward the western sea; in both summer and winter it shall occur. And the LORD shall be King over all the earth. In that day it shall be—"The Lord is one," and His name one. All the land shall be turned into a plain from Geba to Rimmon south of Jerusalem. Jerusalem shall be raised up and inhabited in her place from Benjamin's Gate to the place of the First Gate and the Corner Gate, and from the Tower of Hananel to the king's winepresses. The people shall dwell in it; and no longer shall there be utter destruction, but Jerusalem shall be safely inhabited.*
>
> —14:8-11

That describes the millennial kingdom, which Christ will establish immediately in the wake of His coming. Revelation 20 describes it as a time of unprecedented blessing on the whole world, during which Satan is bound and the redeemed live and reign with Christ on earth.

Isaiah 11:6-9 describes the earthly kingdom in still more graphic terms:

> *"The wolf also shall dwell with the lamb, the leopard shall lie down with the young goat, the calf and the young lion and the fatling together; and a little child shall lead them. The cow and the bear shall graze; their young ones shall lie down together; and the lion shall eat straw like the ox. The nursing child shall play by the cobra's hole, and the weaned child shall put his hand in the viper's den. They shall not hurt nor destroy in all My holy mountain, for the earth shall be full of the knowledge of the LORD as the waters cover the sea."*

Christ will eliminate all disease, drought, floods, crop failures, and hunger. Bad weather and natural disasters will be things of the past. All wars, strife, and persecution will end, and righteousness will rule. What child of God does not long to see such a time?

All kinds of speculative questions arise about the millennial kingdom. If the wicked are all annihilated, with whom is the world populated? The only option would seem to be that the children of the elect remnant who emerge from the Tribulation still alive will repopulate the earth over the thousand-year period.[9]

Why is Satan turned loose at the end of the Millennium and permitted to deceive the nations again (Rev. 20:7-8)? Scripture does not say, but we can be confident that the Lord's purpose is a good one. It certainly will demonstrate that even in a perfect world, people born with depraved hearts cannot ultimately avoid the lure of evil and are desperately in need of redemption.

THE PARABLE OF THE FIG TREE

In the Olivet Discourse, however, Christ spends no time giving details about the millennial kingdom. Once He has reached the zenith of His message, once He has given them the final great sign of the end of the age, He gives a brief parable to underscore the lesson He has been teaching them:

> *"Now learn this parable from the fig tree: When its branch has already become tender and puts forth leaves, you know that summer is near. So you also, when you see all these things, know that it is near—at the doors! Assuredly, I say to you, this generation will by no means pass away till all these things take place. Heaven and earth will pass away, but My words will by no means pass away."*
> —MATT. 24:32-35

Many interpretations have been set forth to try to explain what Jesus meant here. It was popular for some time after the founding of the modern Jewish state to suggest that the fig tree is a reference to modern Israel. Therefore, many believed, from the time the "fig tree" started to bud—meaning 1948, when modern Israel declared statehood—it would be one generation until all the prophecies of the Olivet Discourse were fulfilled. By 1988, when the forty years thought to constitute a "generation" had passed since Israel's founding, that interpretation was not quite so popular.

Some suggest that "this generation" refers not to a particular *age* but rather to the Jewish *race*—employing the word *generation* (much the way Jesus used it in Luke 9:41 and 16:8) to speak of a class of people rather than a period of time. That's a possible interpretation, but it seems to conflict with the context, in which Christ is making a statement about the speed with which all these signs would unfold.

Preterists, of course, place much stress on this verse. They insist it guarantees that the generation alive during Jesus' time would be the same generation to see the complete fulfillment of all these signs, and they treat it as the key that unlocks the meaning of the Olivet Discourse. But the reasonable mind quickly sees the folly of having to allegorize so many passages of Scripture just for the sake of interpreting one verse (v. 34) with such rigid literalism. It is simply not necessary to insist that Christ meant that all the Olivet Discourse signs must be fulfilled in that current generation.

As we have seen throughout our study, many clues in the passage itself, including the cosmic signs and the abomination of desolation, indicate that these are end-time Tribulation prophecies, not merely historical warnings about A.D. 70. Furthermore, Christ says, "When you see *all* these things, know that it is near" (v. 33). The signs are a package. When they are truly fulfilled, they will be fulfilled all at once. That seems to be the gist of this parable, as well as the comment that follows it. Therefore, the most reasonable interpretation of verse 34 is this: Christ is saying that the generation alive when the true labor pains begin will be the same generation that sees the delivery. These things, when they happen, will not stretch out across generations.

In fact, this is the very meaning of the fig tree parable. When the fig tree starts to bud, you can virtually count the days until summer. Likewise, from the time when the actual birth-pang signs begin, there is a set time until all these things will be fulfilled—seven years, to be exact. The Olivet Discourse covers a relatively short period of time, not a long eschatological age. It is essentially a seven-year period, the seventieth week of Daniel's prophecy. And the generation that sees the start of it will be the same one that sees the fulfillment of all the things Christ predicted. So when the real birth-pang signs begin, when that is confirmed by the abomination of desolation and gives way to the trials of the Great Tribulation—"when you see *all* these things"—you can know that Christ's return is near.

The point of the parable is utterly uncomplicated; even a child can tell by looking at a fig tree that summer is near. Likewise, the generation that sees *all* these signs come to pass will know with certainty that Christ's return is near.

This exhortation is reminiscent of a rebuke Christ gave the Pharisees in Matthew 16:2-3: "When it is evening you say, 'It will be fair weather, for the sky is red'; and in the morning, 'It will be foul weather today, for the sky is red and threatening.' Hypocrites! You know how to discern the face of the sky, but you cannot discern the signs of the times."

Those who recognize the signs will realize that Christ's coming is at the door. Those living during the Tribulation can have absolute confidence that He will return soon, despite the viciousness of the persecutions, no matter how convincing the lies of the deceivers, regardless of how much it seems Satan, not God, is in control of things. In Christ's own words, "See, I have told you beforehand" (Matt. 24:25).

The reliability of His prophetic promises is confirmed by the unchanging authority of the Word of God. "Heaven and earth will pass away, but My words will by no means pass away" (v. 35). "The Scripture cannot be broken" (John 10:35). "The grass withers, the flower fades, but the word of our God stands forever" (Isa. 40:8). Therefore, those who are alive when these things come to pass can know with rock-solid certainty that His promises are true. And no matter how bleak things begin to look in the Tribulation, Christ will ultimately emerge as Victor over His enemies.

Seven

DOES ANYBODY REALLY KNOW WHAT TIME IT IS?

Whenever the subject of Christ's return is raised, someone will inevitably ask: *"When* will these things happen?" It's the same question that was on the disciples' lips just before Christ ascended into heaven. His final earthly words to them established an unequivocal boundary we must not attempt to breach: "It is not for you to know times or seasons which the Father has put in His own authority" (Acts 1:7). The precise time is not for us to know. It is the Father's business alone. It is one of those hidden things Scripture instructs us to leave to the secret province of God (Deut. 29:29). It is not something for us to try to discover.

Nevertheless, throughout forty years of preaching I have noticed that whenever I teach on these issues, someone invariably will beg me to speculate about how much time we have left before Christ returns. There seems to be a burning, universal desire among Christians to try to figure out more precisely when these things will begin to come to pass.

But Christ clearly regarded such speculation as sheer folly: "Of that day and hour no one knows, not even the angels of heaven, but My Father only" (Matt. 24:36). God knows the time because He has already established it in His sovereign plan. The when and how of Christ's return were predetermined in the sovereign wisdom of God. But the angels in heaven do not know the time, and even Jesus in His humanity did not have a conscious awareness of the precise time of His return (Mark 13:32).[1] It is only an arrogant disregard for the Word of God that leads people to think God has given them enough clues to figure it out. It is simply not for us to know.

Some point out that Christ already gave several signs that will clearly signal His return. One of the main signs, the abomination of desolation, starts the clock ticking on a catastrophic three-and-a-half year countdown to Christ's final return. Remember that Daniel expressly said, "From the time that the daily sacrifice is taken away, and the abomination of desolation is set up, there shall be one thousand two hundred and ninety days" (Dan. 12:11). So won't it instantly be obvious when the abomination occurs that Christ's return will be three and a half years away? Isn't this virtually the whole point Jesus was making about the abomination of desolation? How does this harmonize with His statement that no one knows the time?

First of all, even with all the signs, the exact day and hour of Christ's coming will not be known. The signs certainly enjoin a more diligent watchfulness as the time approaches, but they do not signify an exact day or hour. Despite all the signs that precede His coming, when Christ appears, most people will still be unprepared for Him. "The Son of Man is coming at an hour you do not expect" (Luke 12:40).

But an even larger principle underlies these words. "That day and hour" may best be understood as a synecdoche that encompasses the whole Second Coming chronology. The question of when *all* these events will begin to happen is deliberately left in the realm of mystery. Christ was therefore forbidding end-time date-setting in general. He was discouraging the disciples, and all of us who live on this side of the Tribulation, from engaging in conjecture or drawing up calendars and time lines. He was reiterating what He invariably taught whenever the subject of His return arose: "It is not for you to know the times or seasons" (Acts 1:7).

He will make this same point several times between Matthew 24:36 and the end of the Olivet Discourse. "Watch therefore, for you do not know what hour your Lord is coming" (24:42). "Be ready, for the Son of Man is coming at an hour you do not expect" (v. 44).

"The master of that servant will come on a day when he is not look-ing for him and at an hour that he is not aware of" (v. 50). "Watch therefore, for you know neither the day nor the hour in which the Son of Man is coming" (25:13).

In all those verses, the terms "day" and "hour" refer not only to the specific moment of His final glorious appearing, but also more broadly to the eschatological time frame in which all these events will unfold. All such admonitions call for a general state of readiness for all believers of all ages. Christ is expressly teaching the truth that we studied in Chapter 2: His coming is imminent.

When we say His coming is imminent, we are speaking in broad terms, of course. His final return in glory is not imminent in the same sense that the Rapture is. There are indeed many signs that must precede His final coming *with* the saints in glory. But the aspect of Christ's return we look for today is the Rapture—His coming *for* the saints (1 Thess. 4:16-17; John 14:3; 1 Cor. 15:51-54). The removal of the church from the world will likely kick off the birth-pang signs and all the rest of the events Christ has outlined so far in His Olivet Discourse. His statement "You do not know what hour your Lord is coming" (v. 42) is therefore as applicable to those of us who await the Rapture as it will be for people in the Tribulation awaiting the consummation, the Second Coming. In one sense the summons to be ready is even *more* applicable to us, because there are no signs whatsoever that will precede the Rapture.

In other words, when Jesus says, "Of that day and hour no one knows" (v. 36), He is teaching a *principle* that applies not only to the moment of His final coming in glory, but also to every aspect of the Bible's Second Coming prophecies. The warning is particularly ger-mane to the Rapture, since the Rapture will inaugurate all the rest of the end-time events, culminating swiftly and finally in Christ's glorious return to earth.

Christ's call to readiness and watchfulness is the central theme of everything that remains in the Olivet Discourse. Everything up to this point has been a graphic narrative about events that will occur in the Tribulation. What remains is the *application* of that earlier part of the discourse. Some might be tempted to limit the immediate application of the second half of the discourse exclusively to that yet-future generation who will find themselves caught up in the Great Tribulation. But that would be a mistake. Christ's appeal here is quite clearly meant for all believers in all ages. Both the spirit and the words of Jesus' statements make this clear. The principle He is teaching certainly applies to all of us. And since He is encouraging His people to be ready and expectant whether He comes or delays, the teaching is as pertinent for those who wait while He delays as it will be for those who witness His sudden coming.

This latter half of the Olivet Discourse is a potent and focused appeal for one thing—preparedness. Every statement and every parable from this point to the end of the discourse contributes to this one simple message: Be ready—Christ is coming when you least expect Him. He highlights four essential virtues believers should cultivate while they wait.

HUMILITY

First, He preemptively punctures the pride of the date-setters. "But of that day and hour no one knows." It takes a certain degree of humility to admit ignorance on such a vital point of major importance. That is why so many of the self-styled "experts" on Bible prophecy insist on speculation and conjecture with regard to dates and times. Their obstinate determination to make guesses about a matter on which Scripture is so decisively silent betrays their own pride. Their tendency to sensationalize their own presumption is even more embarrassing to the cause of Christ.

Why has God kept the timing of Christ's return hidden from the entire church for nearly 2,000 years? I can think of several good reasons.

For one thing, if everyone knew the precise time of Christ's return, no doubt many would be tempted to defer their obedience. If people knew they had exactly ten years before the Rapture, many would imagine they had time to sin for nine and a half years, then plan to repent shortly before Christ comes. (Too many people live their lives that way anyway.) Others would use the approaching end of all things as an excuse for laziness or irresponsibility. Multitudes would no doubt decide to live out the remaining days in lawn chairs on the hillside. These very things happen every time a modern "prophet" announces he has unlocked the secret of the timing of Christ's return. I know of a family who sold their house and all their possessions and took an extended travel vacation because they were convinced Christ was returning on the date one of the recent date-setters had established. When He did not return as expected, this man and his wife had already squandered all their resources and had to start over from scratch. In Chapter 8 we will examine a parable whose very point is to caution us against that kind of foolhardiness.

It is partly because of God's mercy that He keeps hidden from us the timing of Christ's return. If the hour of Christ's coming were known, no one, believer or unbeliever, would be able to maintain a right perspective on the future. It would be impossible to think or function normally. We would lose that balance of both expectancy and patience God commands us to maintain.

Furthermore, it is unnecessary for us to know the timing of Christ's return. Nothing God demands of us necessitates that we know *when* Christ is coming. In fact, our desire should be that He will find us faithful no matter when He comes. If we knew the exact time in advance, it would call our motivation into question and ruin an opportunity to prove that our devotion to Him is pure.

Here's proof of how utterly unnecessary it is for us to know the timing of Christ's return: even the angels are not privy to this secret. "Of that day and hour no one knows, not even the angels in heaven." As we noted above, Mark's account informs us further that Jesus Himself did not know the time: "Of that day and hour no one knows, not even the angels in heaven, nor the Son, but only the Father" (Mark 13:32). In His submission to the Father's will, the omniscient Son had refrained from calling this bit of information to His conscious human mind.

Does anyone imagine that Christ or the angels were uninterested in the exact time of the Second Coming events? Scripture tells us angels have an understandable curiosity about great spiritual truths that God has not fully revealed to them (1 Pet. 1:12). Surely they would want to know *this* truth. After all, they will be directly and actively involved in those end-time events (cf. v. 31). Along with all creation, they are eagerly awaiting the time, groaning and laboring until it comes to pass (Rom. 8:22-23). Even Christ Himself must have had a normal human desire to know the timing of His own return. Yet He humbly submitted to the Father's will in this, as in all matters (John 5:30; 6:38; 8:29).

He demands that same humility from us. This is therefore the starting-point for a proper Second Coming perspective—humility.

ALERTNESS

Christ also calls us to be watchful and expectant. He likens the imminency of His return to the suddenness of the Genesis flood:

> *"But of that day and hour no one knows, not even the angels of heaven, but My Father only. But as the days of Noah were, so also will the coming of the Son of Man be. For as in the days before the flood, they were eating and drinking, marrying and giving in marriage, until the day that Noah entered the ark, and did not know until the flood came and took them all away, so also will the coming of the Son of Man be. Then two men will be in the field: one will be taken and the other left. Two women will be grinding at the mill: one will be taken and the other left. Watch therefore, for you do not know what hour your Lord is coming."*
>
> —MATT. 24:36-42

The Flood is a perfect illustration of Jesus' point. Most people in Noah's day were caught completely off guard, unprepared, not ready. By the time the Flood came and they realized it, it was already too late for them. So shall it be when Christ returns.

We know from the Old Testament that the days of Noah, before the Flood, were days when unbridled wickedness ruled the earth. Genesis 6:5 says of that time, "The LORD saw that the wickedness of man was great in the earth, and that every intent of the thoughts of his heart was only evil continually."

But the point Jesus is making here is not primarily about the extraordinary wickedness of those days. When He says, "they were eating and drinking, marrying and giving in marriage," He is not describing activities that are inherently *sinful*. Rather, these were everyday activities. People were going through the motions of life as usual. The day the rains started, the people of the world ate breakfast as usual. Weddings were scheduled for that very day. There was no preliminary warning, no extended period of gray clouds signaling them that judgment was on the way. The Flood simply came without any prior sign from heaven and swept them all away. They were caught completely by surprise.

"Eating and drinking, marrying and giving in marriage" are the *sensual* aspects of everyday life, however. Their daily lives had degenerated to the point where sensual pursuits were *all* they cared for. Their philosophy of life was precisely what the apostle Paul said is to be expected of someone who has no hope of resurrection: "Let us eat and drink, for tomorrow we die!" (1 Cor. 15:32). They utterly neglected all spiritual duties. They were so caught up with appeasing their sensual appetites that those appetites in effect became the god they worshiped.

Those people were smitten with a sinful spiritual apathy. In their midst lived Noah, whom Peter, writing under the Holy Spirit's inspiration, calls "a preacher of righteousness" (2 Pet. 2:5). Peter also says that "the Divine longsuffering waited in the days of Noah, while the ark was being prepared" (1 Pet. 3:20). Noah was building a massive ark, and that certainly was no secret in his neighborhood. He had found grace in the eyes of the Lord, and he knew the Flood was coming. His very lifestyle stood as a warning to his neighbors, and there is little doubt that this "preacher of righteousness" gave them many verbal warnings too, right up until the day the Lord closed the door of the ark. If the people had listened, if they'd had spiritual ears to hear, they would have received ample warning about the coming flood.

But those heedless, careless people utterly ignored Noah. They went on with life as usual. No doubt many of them lived by the same philosophy as the scoffers in 2 Peter 3:4: "Since the fathers fell asleep, all things continue as they were from the beginning of creation." Life goes on. But only fools imagine it will go on forever. The wise hearer will stay ready, even though we cannot know the precise day and hour.

The average person today is likewise utterly oblivious to the inevitability of Christ's sudden return. Sadly, even many professing Christians live their lives without ever giving a thought to the possibility that they could find themselves in the presence of Christ at any moment. That sort of apathy makes us dull and spiritually sluggish. Christ's aim in this second half of the Olivet Discourse is to move our hearts with a desire to be constantly alert and watchful for His return.

During the Tribulation all humanity will be more sin-hardened and spiritually calloused than ever before. As the crises of the Tribulation become more urgent, and earthly problems begin to assault the simplest aspects of everyday life, people will stubbornly become more and more hostile to God—and more determined than ever to live their lives as usual. Incredibly, with the universe literally collapsing around them, they will keep "eating and drinking, marrying and giving in marriage." The more desperately they need to turn to the Lord, the more impervious they will be to His truth. Though they will suffer the worst imaginable consequences of human sin, they will nonetheless arrogantly refuse to repent (Rev. 9:20-21).

All the perils of the birth pangs, the abomination of desolation, and the signs in the sky will have no effect on the majority of people who live during the Tribulation. Their hearts will be hardened to truth. They will see the signs but will explain them away as natural phenomena. They will hear the Gospel (Matt. 24:14), but they will not *heed* the Gospel. They will have every opportunity to repent.

But they will refuse and go right on "eating and drinking, marrying and giving in marriage," just as in the days of Noah.

As we have seen already, however, a multitude *will* be saved during the Tribulation (Rev. 6:9-11; 7:9-14). Though the era will predominantly be known for sin and unbelief, Israel and a Gentile remnant will be redeemed. And Christ suggests that when He returns, His coming will result in the immediate and irreversible separation of those believers from the unbelievers: "Then two men will be in the field: one will be taken and the other left. Two women will be grinding at the mill: one will be taken and the other left" (vv. 40-41).

This imagery is a comparison to what occurred in Noah's day, when most were taken away by judgment in the Flood, while eight souls were "left" on earth, being saved in the ark (1 Pet. 3:20). Likewise, when Christ returns, some will be judged and some will be saved.

The question of who is "left" and who is "taken" is a point of some debate. Some think this is a reference to the Rapture, and the "taken" ones are the ones who will be saved. But since Christ has said nothing about the Rapture throughout this whole discourse, the context seems to rule out that interpretation.

Puritan commentator Matthew Henry proposed a similar interpretation. He wrote:

He had said before (v. 31), that the elect will be *gathered together*. Here he tells us, that, in order to do that, they will be distinguished from those who were nearest to them in this world; the choice and chosen ones taken to glory, the other left to perish eternally. . . . Christ will come unlooked for, will find people busy at their usual occupations, *in the field, at the mill;* and then, according as they are vessels of mercy prepared for glory, or vessels of wrath prepared for ruin, accordingly it will be with them; the one taken *to meet the Lord and his angels in the air, to be for ever with him and them;* the other left to the devil and his angels, who, when Christ has gathered out his own, will sweep up the residue.[2]

By that interpretation, the one who is "taken" is rescued from destruction and the one who is "left" is left to judgment.

I'm more inclined to think Christ meant that the ones who are "taken" will be taken away by judgment at His return, and the ones who are "left" are people who are left on earth to enter the kingdom. The ones taken are gathered for judgment. They are like the tares that were gathered to be burned. The ones left are like the wheat placed in the barn (Matt. 13:30).

This is the same lesson Christ will elaborate on shortly: the sheep will be separated from the goats (cf. 25:32-46). The return of Christ will mean sudden and permanent separation of the wicked from the redeemed. Christ is emphasizing the urgency of salvation now, during the day of salvation, because the day of opportunity will soon be gone. The door of the ark will be sealed shut, so to speak. It will happen without warning, and the consequences will be instant and irreversible. Don't be caught by surprise. Be on the alert.

Christ makes the point inescapable: "Watch therefore, for you do not know what hour your Lord is coming" (v. 42). The verb tense speaks of a continual watchfulness, a habit of expectancy. There's no latitude for apathy or indifference. The only proper perspective for the Christian is one of hopeful, eager watchfulness.

READINESS

In order to illustrate the statement "you do not know what hour your Lord is coming," Christ likens His coming to the invasion of a thief: "But know this, that if the master of the house had known what hour the thief would come, he would have watched and not allowed his house to be broken into. Therefore you also be ready, for the Son of Man is coming at an hour you do not expect" (vv. 43-44).

If Christ Himself had not employed the expression, it might

seem an impiety to compare His coming to the prowling entry of a common burglar. There certainly is no legitimate comparison between the character of the thief and the sinless Son of God. But there is a valid and vital metaphor involving the secretiveness and suddenness of a thief's arrival, as well as a secondary lesson about the wisdom of the householder. Jesus' twofold point is simple and clear: no thief in his right mind would announce his own coming, and no homeowner in his right mind would leave the house unlocked and unguarded if he knew a thief was coming at a certain hour.

Pursue the metaphor a little further: if the homeowner knows for sure that the thief is coming, even if he does not know the *time* of the thief's arrival, he will be on guard continually and stay prepared for the thief. We know that Christ is coming. We do not know the hour. Therefore it behooves us to be prepared at *all* times.

This imagery of a thief in the night is repeated several times in New Testament teaching about the Second Coming: "You yourselves know perfectly that the day of the Lord so comes as a thief in the night" (1 Thess. 5:2). "The day of the Lord will come as a thief in the night, in which the heavens will pass away with a great noise, and the elements will melt with fervent heat; both the earth and the works that are in it will be burned up" (2 Pet. 3:10). "If you will not watch, I will come upon you as a thief, and you will not know what hour I will come upon you" (Rev. 3:3). "Behold, I am coming as a thief. Blessed is he who watches, and keeps his garments, lest he walk naked and they see his shame" (Rev. 16:15).

Notice how frequently the thief imagery is conjoined to the Day-of-the-Lord judgment. The suddenness, unexpectedness, and finality of Christ's return are among the key factors that make the Day of the Lord such a fearful prospect. And as far as the ungodly are concerned, Christ's coming will be exactly like that of a thief: He will take everything from them.

How should people prepare for the Lord's return? He's calling first of all for a soul-readiness. He is urging people to be reconciled to God. He is talking about instantly separating redeemed people from those who will be damned, and therefore the readiness He is calling for begins with salvation. "Be ready" (v. 44) is virtually an evangelistic appeal to the lost.

Second, He is calling for faithfulness from those who are already redeemed, and the parable He follows up with makes this clear.

FAITHFULNESS

The parable illustrates the statement at the end of verse 44 ("The Son of Man is coming at an hour you do not expect").

> *"Who then is a faithful and wise servant, whom his master made ruler over his household, to give them food in due season? Blessed is that servant whom his master, when he comes, will find so doing. Assuredly, I say to you that he will make him ruler over all his goods. But if that evil servant says in his heart, 'My master is delaying his coming,' and begins to beat his fellow servants, and to eat and drink with the drunkards, the master of that servant will come on a day when he is not looking for him and at an hour that he is not aware of, and will cut him in two and appoint him his portion with the hypocrites. There shall be weeping and gnashing of teeth."*
>
> —24:45-51

The imagery of the parable is obvious. The master represents Christ, the blessed servant represents faithful believers, and the evil servant represents unbelievers. Human life is portrayed as a stewardship in which the servants are given oversight and responsibility for the master's possessions. The master's "goods" are metaphors for the time, talents, resources, and opportunities God entrusts us with. Everything we have was given to us by God (1 Cor. 4:7). We are accountable for how we manage what He gives us, and the time will come when each of us will give an account (Rom. 14:12). In the parable, the return of the master means it is time for the slaves to give account.

The blessed servant is the one found doing what his master had commanded (Matt. 24:46). He is rewarded by being placed in charge of *all* the Master's goods (v. 47). He is given sweeping powers to manage *all* the master's possessions. He is in effect elevated to the highest possible seat of authority and privilege, except for that of the master himself.

That represents believers who are found faithful to the Lord. They will rule and reign with Christ in the kingdom (2 Tim. 2:12; Rev. 20:6). They become joint heirs with Christ (Rom. 8:17), inheriting all the privileges of the kingdom. They are even granted the right to sit with Christ on his throne (Rev. 3:21)!

The evil servant represents an unbeliever. Notice that his heart is devoid of any expectancy about the master's return: he "says in his heart, 'My master is delaying his coming'" (v. 48). And his lack of expectancy gives him a false sense of security in his evil behavior.

The truth portrayed by the evil servant is a very important point: *everyone* will give account to God for the deeds of this life—even people who refuse to acknowledge His existence. He gave them life and all their possessions and all their abilities. They have nothing whatsoever that was not entrusted to them by God. They too are His stewards, albeit unfaithful ones. And He has every right to demand an accounting.

In the parable the master appears suddenly, unexpectedly, catching the evil servant off guard. The nature of the punishment the servant receives proves that he represents an unbeliever. He is cut in two—killed—and consigned to the place of the hypocrites, where according to Jesus, "There shall be weeping and gnashing of teeth" (v. 51). That is an unmistakable reference to hell (cf. 13:42, 50). Here Jesus has slipped out of the language of the parable, which dealt with temporal, earthly realities, and into the language of eternity. He thus made clear the meaning of the parable and emphasized the urgency of the warning He was giving.

"Weeping and gnashing of teeth" is strong imagery. It speaks of the endless sorrow and torment of hell. The "weeping" speaks of grief—personal remorse over squandered opportunities, conscience pangs from the knowledge that one's condemnation is just, anguish from the realization that judgment is final and the day of salvation is past. The "gnashing of teeth" speaks of everlasting torment—unending pain, lostness, and unadulterated woe. Christ often emphasized the utter misery of hell, urging people to flee the wrath to come by being reconciled to God. There is no perverse glee but only sorrow in His descriptions of eternal torment. Nor does He depict hell so graphically for purely academic reasons. There is a gracious purpose in His portraits of everlasting punishment: He is urging His hearers to believe while there is still opportunity. And in this parable in particular He is showing the folly of presuming that the Lord will delay His coming, thus eliminating the urgency of the Gospel.

But the lesson of this parable goes beyond a simple call to faith. It is also a call to *faithfulness.* The blessed servant (vv. 45-47) is a model of the attitude believers should have as they await the Lord's return. He was busy. He was devoted to the task entrusted to him. He was loyal. He was obedient. And when the master returned unexpectedly, this servant was ready—because he had *stayed* ready the whole time the master was away. His employer could have returned at any time, and he would have found this servant faithful. The servant did not view his master's absence as an opportunity to declare an unauthorized sabbatical for himself. Quite the opposite. He took his responsibility seriously and stayed faithfully at the task. He regarded the master's absence as all the more reason to remain diligent.

That is the proper mind-set for the expectant Christian. Our Lord's delay does not mean there is no urgency about His coming. We dare not grow lax or lazy. Above all, we cannot lose our sense of watchful expectancy. He *is* coming. He might delay even longer, or He could come today. Either way, He should find us alert and prepared and faithful.

Eight

THE DANGER OF
FOOLISH EXPECTATIONS

The parable at the end of Matthew 24 and the parable at the start of Matthew 25 make an interesting contrast. The two parables teach opposite but complementary lessons. The parable about the servants (24:45-51) teaches us to be prepared for Christ in case He comes sooner than we think He will. The parable of the virgins (25:1-13) teaches us to be prepared in case He *delays* longer than expected. Both attitudes are absolutely essential to a balanced biblical hope.

As we discussed in the previous chapter, people who have no expectancy of Christ's imminent return are inclined to develop careless spiritual habits. They become preoccupied with worldly things and grow apathetic about spiritual matters.

But the opposite error poses equal dangers. Lots of people fix a time frame in their minds beyond which they presume Christ could not possibly tarry. That establishes an artificial boundary for all their plans, preparations, and aspirations. They never look beyond their arbitrary deadline. They therefore have an unwise and reckless view of the future. In effect, they also impose a false time limit on hope itself—and many who fall into this error finally lose heart when their expectations are not met. The epidemic of high-profile date-setters over the past couple of decades has left thousands of disillusioned people with shattered expectations.

That's because such expectations are utterly foolish in the first place. Nothing in Scripture promises us Christ will return by any chronological deadline known to us. In fact, we are repeatedly told that we do not know the day or the hour He is coming. That truth is expressly stated at least five times in the Olivet Discourse (24:36, 42, 44, 50; 25:13). So it is sheer presumption to fix a time frame in our minds and live by the assumption that Christ cannot possibly delay His coming beyond that date.

The explicit date-setters are not the only ones who make this error. I know people who are reaching retirement age right now without having set aside any savings or retirement pension because in the 1960s and 1970s they read all the then-popular books implying that the Rapture was going to happen within twenty years, if not sooner. These people had witnessed the formation of Israel as a nation. They sensed the rise of hostility between the world's super-powers, much of it focused on the Middle East. They kept hearing self-styled Bible prophecy experts speak about the "fulfillment" of this or that biblical sign. And they foolishly concluded there was no way they would ever reach retirement age before the Rapture; so they did not even prepare for the possibility. It never occurred to them that Christ could delay longer than they envisioned.

By their own testimony, many of the people now touting hyper-preterism—denying any future return of Christ whatsoever—are people who once devoured all the best sellers on Bible prophecy and were certain Christ would return before the end of the millennium. They became disillusioned when those expectations turned out to be false.

But those are precisely the sort of foolish expectations this parable warns against.

The hope of Christ's return per se certainly is not foolish. As we have seen throughout our study of the Second Coming, a mind-set of constant expectation and hope for His imminent coming is the very thing Scripture commands of us. But to presume that we know *when* He's coming—or even to shape our planning and preparation for the future according to an approximate time frame in which we think He surely *must* return—is to entertain a foolish expectation.

With all Jesus' stress on the imminency of His coming and the urgency of being ready, He does not neglect to emphasize the balancing truth as well: faithful Christians should remain patient, even if He delays longer than we think possible. We should remain prepared, keep preparing for the future, and go on living life while we wait. We don't show our readiness for His coming by going to a hillside somewhere to wait idly for Him to appear. While we wait, we are to go about doing His business and spreading the Gospel on earth with long-suffering, patience, and earnest devotion, not despairing or losing an ounce of our hope if He delays His coming.

Jesus illustrates the point with a parable about a wedding ceremony:

> *"Then the kingdom of heaven shall be likened to ten virgins who took their lamps and went out to meet the bridegroom. Now five of them were wise, and five were foolish. Those who were foolish took their lamps and took no oil with them, but the wise took oil in their vessels with their lamps. But while the bridegroom was delayed, they all slumbered and slept. And at midnight a cry was heard: 'Behold, the bridegroom is coming; go out to meet him!' Then all those virgins arose and trimmed their lamps. And the foolish said to the wise, 'Give us some of your oil, for our lamps are going out.' But the wise answered, saying, 'No, lest there should not be enough for us and you; but go rather to those who sell, and buy for yourselves.' And while they went to buy, the bridegroom came, and those who were ready went in with him to the wedding; and the door was shut. Afterward the other virgins came also, saying, 'Lord, Lord, open to us!' But he answered and said, 'Assuredly, I say to you, I do not know you.' Watch therefore, for you know neither the day nor the hour in which the Son of Man is coming."*
>
> —MATT. 25:1-13

Here is a nighttime wedding ceremony where everything seems to go wrong. The bridegroom is tardy. The bridesmaids get drowsy. The lamps go out. Half the wedding party misses the start of the ceremony and ends up being banned by the bridegroom. Can you imagine a more disastrous wedding?

But each phase of this apparent wedding fiasco holds a lesson about the coming of the heavenly Bridegroom.

THE BRIDEGROOM IS TARDY

The first thing to notice is the belated arrival of the bridegroom. Why he is so late is not explained. Apparently he was coming from a far distance. Perhaps weather or other circumstances hindered him. Whatever the reason for his delay, he arrived later than anyone would have thought possible. In fact, it was probably starting to look like he might not show up at all. Even the wedding party fell asleep waiting for him. He did not arrive until midnight—several hours after the wedding ceremony would typically have been scheduled to begin.

This was not a deliberate slight. He "was delayed" (v. 5). It was an unavoidable delay of some kind. From his determination to get on with the wedding once he arrived, we can deduce that his tardiness was not owing to any indecision or hesitancy on his part about the wedding plans. The long delay doesn't suggest that he was unenthusiastic about the wedding feast. It doesn't insinuate any defect in his love for the bride. He doubtless had good reasons for the delay, even though his reasons are not explained as a part of the parable.

Any bridegroom *that* late for a modern wedding in our culture would no doubt find everyone gone home and the wedding called off, period. But this was a different sort of wedding ceremony than what we are accustomed to in a modern Western culture.

You'll recall our discussion in chapter 1 about marriages in biblical times. The typical Jewish marriage was a three-part event, spread out over many months. Step 1 was a legal engagement contract, usually arranged by the parents and sealed with the payment of a bridal price. Step 2 was the betrothal period, launched by a public ceremony where vows and gifts were exchanged. Betrothal could last for as much as a year, and during that time the new husband was responsible to demonstrate that he could make a livelihood. He also used the betrothal period to build a home where the couple would start their lives together. During betrothal the marriage was fully binding and could be dissolved only by divorce, even though the physical union of the couple was not yet consummated. Step 3 was a wedding banquet, held at the end of the betrothal period. The banquet was usually held at the bride's home. Only after the wedding banquet did the bride return to her husband's home, and then the union was finally consummated.

The ceremony described in the parable is the wedding banquet, the final stage in the marriage festivities. Marriage banquets were community celebrations that often lasted as much as a whole week. At the start of the celebration, the bridegroom and his groomsmen would go to the bride's house. His arrival was a ceremonial event, heralded by the bridesmaids, who would come out to meet the bridegroom and escort him to the bride's house. On the way, however, the whole wedding party would wend their way through the streets of the community, proclaiming to all that the wedding feast was about to begin. Such ceremonies were often held at night; so the bride's attendants carried torches. These both lighted the way and added to the pageantry.

And often, especially if the bridegroom was coming from a distance, the precise time of his arrival could not be known in advance. Everyone in the community would know that a wedding feast was imminent. They knew also that the arrival of the bridegroom would officially signal the start of the wedding. But waiting for the bridegroom could be a drawn-out affair. Therefore people went about their normal business until they heard the joyous procession of the wedding party. That was the official announcement in the community that the bridegroom had finally arrived and the banquet was beginning.

In any culture midnight would be considered too late an hour to begin a wedding feast. Even in Jesus' day the wedding festivities would probably be postponed until the next day if the bridegroom hadn't arrived by the middle of the night. Instead of arriving at midnight the bridegroom would probably spend the night just outside of town, postponing his arrival at the bride's house a few more hours in order to finish the journey at a morning hour when people were awake and ready to participate in the pageantry.

But the bridegroom in this parable had waited long enough for his bride. Having already been unavoidably delayed in his journey to the marriage feast, he was not postponing the banquet one moment longer for *any* reason. He had probably sent messengers ahead to inform the wedding party that he had been detained but was still coming, letting them know that even though he was late, once he arrived, the wedding would proceed regardless of the hour. If that meant fewer guests would come because most were home in bed, so be it. But the bridegroom had a right to expect that the wedding party would be faithful enough to stay awake and watch for him.

The central message of this parable is obvious: Christ is coming. He may delay longer than we expect; so we need to make preparations in case that happens. And we must stay alert, even if the hour seems late—because when He *does* arrive, there will be no further delays and no second chances.

In other words, true readiness for Christ's return involves not only the hope that He will appear soon, but also the patience to wait faithfully, without losing hope, so that no matter how long He delays, we remain faithful, alert, and expectant.

THE BRIDESMAIDS GET DROWSY

Again, in order to understand the gist of this parable, we must do our best to see it in the context of first-century Jewish culture. To modern western ears at first hearing, it sounds like the bridegroom spoiled the wedding by being so late. Given the cultural context, however, it is clear that the bridegroom was the one most eager for the wedding to occur. Having been unavoidably detained, he nonetheless wanted to go ahead with the wedding despite the lateness of the hour. The bridesmaids were the ones who ruined the ceremony.

The bridesmaids are called "virgins" because custom held that bridesmaids were always chaste young maidens who had never been married. There were ten of them, all deemed maids of honor. In our culture that would be a very large wedding party, but it is likely that in weddings of that day ten bridesmaids were the minimum. By similar principles, a minimum of ten men were required to establish a synagogue, ten witnesses were required to seal an important contract (cf. Ruth 4:2), and ten persons were always present to witness every circumcision.

The bridesmaids here represent professing believers. Notice that all of them are taken by surprise at the bridegroom's coming after such a long delay, and only half of them are ready for him in *any* sense when he comes. The other five were not prepared for his coming at all, so he banned them from the wedding feast altogether.

The five bridesmaids who were prepared for the bridegroom represent true believers. The five foolish bridesmaids represent professing Christians whose hope of Christ's coming, like the "faith" they profess, is only superficial, temporary, and artificial. In other words, the five foolish bridesmaids represent people who do not truly know the Lord (cf. v. 12). Their expectations about Christ are not grounded in Scripture; so those expectations eventually go unmet. When that occurs, they suffer spiritual shipwreck, and as a result they will not be prepared to meet Christ when He appears.

We might say that the lamp each virgin carried pictures her outward identity with Christ or her testimony for Him. In the imagery of this parable, those whose lamps burn out and cannot be re-lit for lack of fuel signify people who fail to persevere in the faith and thereby demonstrate that they were never truly redeemed in the first place (cf. 1 John 2:19).

Some further suggest that the oil signifies the indwelling Holy Spirit, or the saving grace of God. (Others say the oil is the Word of God, and the light given off by the torch is the light of the Gospel.) But spelling out the meaning of each detail of the parable isn't really necessary. In fact, it is never wise to try to wring too much significance out of the secondary details of a parable. Parables are not allegories, where every feature has some symbolic or mystical meaning. Parables are simple illustrations, and in most cases they convey just one central lesson. This one main point always lies in the precept taught by the parable, not in the secondary details. Many people try so hard to extract meaning from details in parables that they miss the simple, central lesson.

In this parable the lesson is entirely straightforward: Since you do not know the time, Christ may come later than you think. Stay ready in case He delays.

The "lamps" spoken of in the parable are really torches. The Greek term is *lampas*. It is the same word from which the English word *lamp* is derived, but in the New Testament it normally signifies a torch. (Cf. John 18:3, where *phanos* is used for "lantern" and *lampas* is "torch." *Luchnos* was the New Testament term for a lamp.) These were ceremonial torches, used for decorative purposes as well as for light. They were long, colorful poles with wick-fabric wrapped tightly around the top. The fabric was saturated with oil, which burnt brightly. When the oil was consumed, the fabric would merely smolder and go out; so it was important to keep the torches well-saturated with oil.

Half the bridesmaids in this parable were "wise." They brought flasks with extra oil in case their torches needed additional fuel. Five of the bridesmaids were "foolish," however, and gave no thought to the possibility that they might need their torches to burn longer than expected. They brought no extra oil.

The torches were probably sufficiently supplied with oil for the wedding procession through the streets. So the foolish virgins might have had no need for additional fuel if the ceremony had started at an earlier hour. But as the evening wore on and the darkness became deeper, the bridesmaids evidently used their torches to provide light while they waited. It's not hard to picture a houseful of giddy teenage girls, waiting for their friend's wedding, heedlessly burning up the oil in their torches while they chattered on into the night.

But then they began to get drowsy and fall asleep. The hour was late, so their fatigue is somewhat understandable. It shouldn't be interpreted as mere laziness. However, knowing that the bridegroom was definitely coming, and being unsure of *when* He would arrive, someone should have been watching for Him. There was no excuse for the entire wedding party to be so inattentive. But "they all slumbered and slept" (v. 5), even the wise virgins.

THE TORCHES GO OUT

The sleeping bridesmaids were awakened by a shout at midnight: "Behold, the bridegroom is coming; go out to meet him!" They knew this announcement was coming. They were gathered at the bride's house to wait for this very moment. Their one focus should have been on watching and waiting for the bridegroom. Yet inexplicably, when the time finally came, it caught them completely by surprise. So shall it be with the return of Christ.

Suddenly it was time for the wedding procession. They had known it was coming. They should have been ready, but not one bridesmaid was fully prepared. "All those virgins arose and trimmed their lamps" (v. 7). The lamps should have already been trimmed and ready for the ceremony, but evidently they had been left burning and had burned out when all the bridesmaids fell asleep. Trimming them now involved clipping off the ragged and blackened bits of wick-cloth and saturating the torch with fresh oil to prepare it for relighting.

Not until that crucial moment did the foolish bridesmaids realize their predicament. They had no oil. They had no means of relighting their burnt-out torches. They had given no thought to what might happen if the bridegroom was delayed and their torches burnt out. Now suddenly he had appeared, and it was already too late to do anything about it.

The foolish bridesmaids desperately tried to get oil from the prudent bridesmaids. Half the bridesmaids had no oil whatsoever. If they all tried to share the available oil, there simply would not be enough to light all the torches (v. 9). So the wise bridesmaids urged the others to "go rather to those who sell, and buy for yourselves" (v. 9). Shops where oil was sold were generally homes with storefronts. At this hour the bridesmaids would have to find a merchant whom they could awaken and get him to agree to sell them oil despite the lateness of the hour.

They were in a hopeless and irremediable predicament. Without oil they could not participate in the procession. But if they went to get oil, they would miss the arrival of the bridegroom. They opted for the latter, perhaps thinking the bridegroom could be persuaded to wait for them to return before going ahead with the procession.

HALF THE WEDDING PARTY MISSES THE CEREMONY

When the bridegroom arrived, he was apparently unwilling to delay the wedding any longer just to accommodate five foolish bridesmaids. "And those who were ready went in with him to the wedding; and the door was shut" (v. 10). In other words, when the foolish virgins came back from their quest for midnight oil, they found they had already missed the procession—their part in the wedding—and now they were missing the feast too. The banquet was well underway already, and a locked door completely barred their entry. So they began pleading with the bridegroom to let them in.

But they had already ruined the processional ceremony, and he would not now permit them to disrupt the banquet too. "He answered and said, 'Assuredly, I say to you, I do not know you'" (v. 12). Thus they were excluded from the celebration they should have been part of, because of their own foolish lack of preparation.

They had taken for granted that the bridegroom would arrive early. They were not prepared for his delay. They lost focus and fell asleep when they should have been watching, and by the time they awoke it was already too late.

All of that pictures the folly of not being prepared when the heavenly Bridegroom delays His return. The foolish virgins represent people who profess faith in Christ but are not really prepared to wait and watch for Him if it means being committed for the long haul. They may be giddy and excited about the Lord's return as long as they think it will happen within a very short time span. But they are not prepared to wait patiently if He delays beyond what they expect. They quickly grow weary while the Bridegroom tarries. They lose their watchful expectancy. They become discouraged or spiritually sluggish. They ultimately give up hope altogether.

The parable is a warning about short-term or superficial faith (cf. Matt. 13:18-22) and thus is a reminder that many people who fancy themselves followers of Christ and profess to know Him will ultimately be shut out of heaven. Christ warned of this repeatedly during his earthly ministry. The five virgins excluded from the marriage feast represent people who at the judgment will insist they belong in heaven, only to be decisively shut out by Christ with those chilling words, "I never knew you." He drew a similar picture, employing strikingly similar language, in Luke 13:24-28:

> "Strive to enter through the narrow gate, for many, I say to you, will seek to enter and will not be able. When once the Master of the house has risen up and shut the door, and you begin to stand outside and knock at the door, saying, 'Lord, Lord, open for us,' and He will answer and say to you, 'I do not know you, where you are from,' then you will begin to say, 'We ate and drank in Your presence, and You taught in our streets.' But He will say, 'I tell you I do not know you, where you are from. Depart from Me, all you workers of iniquity.' There will be weeping and gnashing of teeth, when you see Abraham and Isaac and Jacob and all the prophets in the kingdom of God, and yourselves thrust out."

Imagine the sheer terror that will fill the hearts and minds of people who thought they were eternally secure merely because they *professed* faith in Christ or did certain works on His behalf or associated with His people via church membership or some other merely external attachment. Their situation will be hopeless, incurable, and irreversible. Christ vividly pictured the scene near the end of His Sermon on the Mount:

> *"Not everyone who says to Me, 'Lord, Lord,' shall enter the kingdom of heaven, but he who does the will of My Father in heaven. Many will say to Me in that day, 'Lord, Lord, have we not prophesied in Your name, cast out demons in Your name, and done many wonders in Your name?' And then I will declare to them, 'I never knew you; depart from Me, you who practice lawlessness!'"*
> —MATT. 7:21-23

The five foolish virgins in this parable epitomize people who will be caught unawares by the judgment that will destroy them. Unable to maintain *any* hope when their original foolish expectations go unmet, they fall away, becoming spiritually lethargic or consumed by immediate things rather than eternal values. Their failure to be patient and stay prepared while the Bridegroom tarries will ultimately cost them everything. Jesus warned against this very tendency:

> *"Take heed to yourselves, lest your hearts be weighed down with carousing, drunkenness, and cares of this life, and that Day come on you unexpectedly. For it will come as a snare on all those who dwell on the face of the whole earth. Watch therefore, and pray always that you may be counted worthy to escape all these things that will come to pass, and to stand before the Son of Man."*
> —LUKE 21:34-36

The parable of the ten virgins may have been a hint to the disciples that Christ would not be returning as quickly as they expected (cf. Luke 19:11). It is unlikely that *any* of them expected Him to tarry 2,000 years, however. In a similar sense, it certainly appears today that the return of Christ must be very near, even at the door. But amid all the hype and sensationalism about Christ's return, we need to remind ourselves that we do not actually know the day or the hour. Christ could *still* tarry longer than we imagine possible. And if He does, we need to remain watchful and expectant—while staying busy and being faithful to the work He has given us to do.

Our Lord has one more parable left to give in the Olivet Discourse, and it is a parable about this very subject of remaining busy and faithful until His appearing.

Nine

THE TRAGEDY OF
WASTED OPPORTUNITY

As we wait for the Lord to return, we can't be standing on our tiptoes every moment looking into heaven. Life has to go on. This is the very point of the parable of the ten virgins: Christ could delay His return, and if so, we must maintain our hope, keep watching for Him, and meanwhile carry on serving Him faithfully. Those who fail to take into account that the Lord may delay longer than we anticipate will eventually be caught unprepared when an unplanned-for future catches up with them. Then when the Lord *does* return, they will be ashamed (cf. 1 John 2:28).

The only way we can make sure we are ready for the Lord's return is to *stay* ready every day. Common sense should teach us that this is the only proper perspective on the future anyway. After all, we do not know when we are going to die. That could happen at any time, even if the Lord does delay His return another generation. We need to be prepared at any time for death as well as for the Lord's return, for we shall face immediate judgment either way. "It is appointed for men to die once, but after this the judgment" (Heb. 9:27). Staying prepared for the Lord's return will therefore ready us to face death too.

Meanwhile, we should live our lives and do our work and plan for the future with wisdom and godly discretion. Those who think the Lord's imminent return cancels out the need for wise planning don't understand what Scripture demands of us.

The necessity of prudent planning is a constant theme in

Scripture. "In the morning sow your seed, and in the evening do not withhold your hand; for you do not know which will prosper, either this or that, or whether both alike will be good" (Eccl. 11:6).

We often hear supercilious church members denigrate planning for the future as if it were antithetical to "walking by faith." But what such people think of as "faith," Scripture reckons as foolishness. Jesus said, "Which of you, intending to build a tower, does not sit down first and count the cost, whether he has enough to finish it— lest, after he has laid the foundation, and is not able to finish, all who see it begin to mock him, saying, 'This man began to build and was not able to finish'" (Luke 14:28-30). It is right to plan, to prepare, and to strategize for the future. Solomon wrote, "He who gathers in summer is a wise son; he who sleeps in harvest is a son who causes shame" (Prov. 10:5).

It is especially essential that we remain diligent, hard-working, and resourceful while we await the Lord's return. The fact that Christ could return at any moment is no excuse for quitting what God has called us to be and do. The day may indeed be drawing very near, but now is not the time to put on our pajamas and sit on the roof! This is no time to fold up our things and retire from all Christian service to await the Lord's appearing. Quite the opposite. The knowledge that Christ could appear at any time is a great incentive to work harder, apply ourselves more diligently, and stay faithfully at the task. The day of opportunity may be short. The time is certainly drawing closer. We dare not squander the opportunity we have left. We must heed Jesus' words: "A little while longer the light is with you. Walk while you have the light, lest darkness overtake you; he who walks in darkness does not know where he is going. While you have the light, believe in the light, that you may become sons of light" (John 12:35-36).

The apostle Paul called us to look for our Lord's return when he wrote:

> *Behold, I tell you a mystery: We shall not all sleep, but we shall all be changed; in a moment, in the twinkling of an eye, at the last trum-*

pet. For the trumpet will sound, and the dead will be raised incorruptible, and we shall be changed. For this corruptible must put on incorruption, and this mortal must put on immortality. So when this corruptible has put on incorruption, and this mortal has put on immortality, then shall be brought to pass the saying that is written: "Death is swallowed up in victory."

1 COR. 15:51-54

But he immediately added, "Therefore, my beloved brethren, be steadfast, immovable, always abounding in the work of the Lord, knowing that your labor is not in vain in the Lord" (v. 58).

The two parables we have just examined (the parable of the two servants in Matthew 24:45-51 and the parable of the ten virgins in 25:1-13) both deal with the tragedy of wasted opportunity. Now our Lord delves even more deeply into this subject in the third of this triptych of parables from the Olivet Discourse. We have come to the familiar parable of the talents (25:14-30), in which a wealthy man takes a journey, giving each of his servants a number of talents to manage until he returns. Two of the servants invest and double the resources they were given stewardship of. The third buries his talent in the ground and does nothing productive with it. The imagery is quite similar to the parable of the two servants at the end of chapter 24, which we have already examined.[1]

This parable and the two preceding ones round out the full picture of what it means to be ready for Christ's return. The parable of the two servants teaches us to show our readiness for Christ's return with an attitude of *expectantly watching* for Him. The parable of the virgins urges us to prove our readiness for Christ by *patiently waiting*. This parable teaches us to remain ready for Him by *diligently working*.

Unfortunately, much of the popular teaching about the Lord's return upsets the balance of those attitudes. Sensationalist approaches to Bible prophecy use hype and exaggeration to motivate people to remain watchful, but in the process the aspects of waiting and working often get short shrift. Where expectancy is heightened, patience is often lacking. Frankly, all of us find it difficult to maintain the necessary balance. That is why Christ took such care to illustrate each of the necessary balancing perspectives.

Maintaining the proper balance was evidently something of a struggle in the early church too. The apostle Paul had to correct an imbalance in the Thessalonian church. The believers there had heard that the Lord was coming soon, and many of them expected Him momentarily. That caused them to become careless and undisciplined in their daily lives. Some of them evidently gave up doing any work at all. They became busybodies, and they were a serious disruption to the rest of the church. In 2 Thessalonians 3:10-15, Paul rebuked them severely and commanded the rest of the church to discipline them if they did not change their ways. He reminded them:

> *Even when we were with you, we commanded you this: If anyone will not work, neither shall he eat. For we hear that there are some who walk among you in a disorderly manner, not working at all, but are busybodies. Now those who are such we command and exhort through our Lord Jesus Christ that they work in quietness and eat their own bread. But as for you, brethren, do not grow weary in doing good. And if anyone does not obey our word in this epistle, note that person and do not keep company with him, that he may be ashamed. Yet do not count him as an enemy, but admonish him as a brother.*

The latter-day mockers described in 2 Peter 3:3-4 suffer from the opposite problem. They think the Lord's long delay means He is *not* coming back.

The challenge for the true believer is to maintain the proper balance of all three perspectives—watching, waiting, and working. The parable of the talents emphasizes the aspect of working. It illustrates four essential points about our stewardship while we await the return of Christ: the responsibility we receive, the reaction we have, the reckoning we will face, and the reward we will gain.

The Responsibility We Receive

The parable pictures a man (evidently a wealthy man) who is making preparations for a long journey: "For the kingdom of heaven is like a man traveling to a far country, who called his own servants and delivered his goods to them. And to one he gave five talents, to another two, and to another one, to each according to his own ability; and immediately he went on a journey" (Matt. 25:14-15).

The imagery is clear. The man going on the journey represents Christ. The time he is away on his journey pictures the time between Christ's ascension into heaven and His bodily return. The servants are professing believers. The talents represent a wide range of spiritual opportunities, privileges, and resources, including natural abilities,[2] spiritual gifts, material things, ministry responsibilities, and other blessings God has given us as stewards. And He will eventually call us to account for that stewardship.

In the parable the fact that this man had three slaves who acted as his stewards suggests that he was immensely wealthy. The slaves entrusted with this responsibility were not common laborers but educated servants who had shown shrewd business abilities. They correspond to upper-level corporate employees in modern culture. They would have been well-educated and highly skilled in the master's affairs. In effect he gave them power of attorney to act on his behalf with regard to the possessions he entrusted to them. Their duty was to *manage* the master's wealth, not merely hold it for him until he returned.

A talent is a measure of weight, not a coin or currency denomination. We're not told whether these were talents of gold or talents of silver (because the actual value is immaterial to Jesus' point). Either way, however, the talent was a large measure; so a large responsibility, and a large monetary value, was given to each of the three stewards. The talents would be weighed and put into bags. One bag weighed five talents, another two, and the third one.

Notice that the master gave the stewards responsibility in keeping with their abilities. The man with the greatest potential received the greatest responsibility. The owner knew his slaves intimately, and he carefully gave each man only the level of responsibility he knew he could be accountable for. There's probably no special significance in the fact that Jesus mentions only three levels of responsibility here. In the nearly identical parable of the minas in Luke 19, the nobleman calls ten servants and gives them ten equal shares of money. Here Christ expressly states that this man gave his slaves responsibility commensurate with their abilities. The fact that all three received differing amounts seems to suggest only that everyone is differently skilled or gifted. In a church of 600 people, there can be 600 different levels of spiritual ability. And God entrusts different levels of responsibility to each person, depending on our giftedness. God knows intimately our abilities because He is the one who has sovereignly gifted us for service (cf. 1 Cor. 4:7), and He graciously assigns our responsibilities accordingly.

THE REACTION WE HAVE

The response of the three servants reveals each one's true character. "Then he who had received the five talents went and traded with them, and made another five talents. And likewise he who had received two gained two more also. But he who had received one went and dug in the ground, and hid his lord's money" (25:16-18).

Two slaves were faithful, embraced the responsibility they had been given, and set to work. The third slave was both lazy and unprincipled. He did nothing with his master's money. He buried it in the ground and either remained idle or took advantage of his master's absence to pursue his own self-interests.

The two faithful servants represent genuine believers whose supreme desire is to serve God. The third servant represents someone who pretends loyalty to Christ but in reality squanders spiritual opportunity, declines to serve the Lord, and serves himself instead.

The trading done by these servants involved investment of the master's resources, not at all unlike the trading that takes place in the stock market today. The verb tenses used suggest they were trading the whole time of the master's absence; they did not merely make one successful trade and then sit idle the rest of the time. They were trading and re-trading as long as the owner was away.

Their trading met with good success; both managed to double their investment while the master was away. The slave who started with five gained five more, and the slave who started with two gained two more. Although one slave was originally given less and therefore had less to work with, he was equally diligent, and his diligence paid off in an equal proportion.

The third slave, however, simply buried his talent. Perhaps he originally planned to dig it up later and try to cover his indolence with some last-minute investing but just never got around to it. Or maybe he hoped the slaves who invested would *lose* money and he would come off looking good by comparison. Whatever he was thinking, it is obvious that he was more interested in doing whatever *he* wanted to do than in fulfilling his duty to the master.

But hiding his master's talent in the ground was a guarantee that those resources would never earn any profit. His behavior was "wicked" (v. 26). He showed great disregard for his duty to the master. He had not been given the money to guard it or hide it but to put it to work for the master's good. Instead, he chose to ignore his duty and to behave as if he were not even accountable to the master. But he would face a reckoning when the master returned.

The Reckoning We Will Face

The master was gone "a long time" (v. 19). Perhaps the servant who buried the talent began to think his master would not return. The longer the master delayed, the more comfortable the unfaithful servant felt in his disobedience. But the master *did* finally return, and evidently he returned suddenly and unexpectedly. Upon his arrival the stewards were all summoned to give account.

> *After a long time the lord of those servants came and settled accounts with them. So he who had received five talents came and brought five other talents, saying, "Lord, you delivered to me five talents; look, I have gained five more talents besides them." His lord said to him, "Well done, good and faithful servant; you were faithful over a few things, I will make you ruler over many things. Enter into the joy of your lord." He also who had received two talents came and said, "Lord, you delivered to me two talents; look, I have gained two more talents besides them." His lord said to him, "Well done, good and faithful servant; you have been faithful over a few things, I will make you ruler over many things. Enter into the joy of your lord."*
>
> —VV. 19-23

Notice that the reckoning is not a contest to see who had earned the largest amount. Though one man earned five talents and the other two, they both earned the same rate of return. Their profits were widely differing sums, but the percentage of profit was the same. Entrusted with unequal amounts in the first place, they had shown a similar faithfulness in how they managed their respective stewardships. And they both received exactly the same praise and the same reward from the master—the man with two talents no less than the five-talent steward.

Likewise, in the eternal reckoning many believers who may have had lowly positions and meager abilities on earth will be praised and rewarded for being faithful with what they had. They will be elevated to positions alongside equally faithful Christians who had greater abilities and therefore accomplished more spectacular things. If the level of faithfulness is the same, the reward will be the same. The slightly-gifted day laborer who lives a faithful life and wins his neighbors and family to Christ will hear the same "Well done!" as the supremely gifted preacher who was also faithful and was used by God to win thousands to Christ. "Each one will receive his own reward according to his own labor" (1 Cor. 3:8)—not according to the results.

Notice that the master's response to the two faithful servants was gracious, kind, and generous. Notice, too, that the servants' reward was an expanded sphere of service. Because they had made the most of an opportunity to serve him, he rewarded them with *more* opportunity to serve, and this was an opportunity of the most joyous kind: "Enter into the joy of your lord" (Matt. 25:21, 23).

That is a picture of heaven, which will be filled with even greater opportunities for service than we can possibly imagine here on earth. But heaven's service will be utterly devoid of the drudgery and toil we often associate with our earthly labors. That sphere of service will be filled with unadulterated joy—the joy of the Lord.

The master's response, "I will make you ruler over many things" (vv. 21, 23), evokes the same idea conveyed in Jesus' promise to the church at Laodicea: "To him who overcomes I will grant to sit with Me on My throne" (Rev. 3:21). That suggests that we will be joint rulers with Christ, not only in the earthly millennial kingdom, but also in some sense in the King's eternal realm. To the disciples, just before His arrest, Christ said, "You are those who have continued with Me in My trials. And I bestow upon you a kingdom, just as My Father bestowed one upon Me" (Luke 22:28-29). So earthly faithfulness results in heavenly reward, and the heavenly reward involves an expanded sphere of service, joint authority with Christ, and the undiluted joy of heaven. Several of Jesus' parables made a similar point (cf. Matt. 24:47; Luke 12:44; 19:17-19).

Heaven will not be boring. The service we render to Christ there will be filled with unimaginable delights. Finally loosed from the tyranny of sin, we will find our service to Christ the most pleasurable, lively, joyous privilege imaginable. Christ Himself suggests this when He has the master in the parable say, "Enter into the joy of your lord." The joy is as much a part of the faithful servants' reward as the increased sphere of service.

But for unfaithful stewards, the story is dramatically different. In Jesus' parable, the character of the third slave is clearly revealed in his reply to the master: "Then he who had received the one talent came and said, 'Lord, I knew you to be a hard man, reaping where you have not sown, and gathering where you have not scattered seed. And I was afraid, and went and hid your talent in the ground. Look, there you have what is yours'" (vv. 24-25). This is an incredibly brash and arrogant reply. He seems to be trying to turn away the master's displeasure by preempting it with a deliberate slur against the master's character. He portrays his master as an unprincipled opportunist with a cruel streak—someone who reaps and gathers what he has no right to. And then he excuses his own inactivity by blaming it on fear caused by the master's "hard" demeanor. In other words, according to this slave, the real fault lies with the master. Instead of giving account, he was making an accusation.

It was a wicked and false accusation. It is obvious that the master was a gracious and generous man. He required of his servants only what he had every right to require—that they be faithful in carrying out the duties he had delegated to them. The servant's accusation merely proves that he had no real knowledge of the master.

His excuse was, moreover, a total lie. He didn't hide that money in the ground because he feared his master; he buried it because it got in the way of his selfish lifestyle. He had no interest in increasing his master's wealth. He was not committed to the honor and glory of his master by extending the master's realm. On the other hand, he had things *he* wanted to do, and as long as the master was not around to hold him accountable, he was perfectly happy to pursue his own interests and utterly neglect his duties. The real problem was that he was lazy and selfish and cared nothing about his duty to the master.

The lie was exposed by the unfaithful servant's own words. He claimed he feared the master because the master was so shrewd, harsh, and demanding. Yet he buried the talent in the ground, where it was guaranteed to earn exactly nothing. He had deliberately and knowingly squandered every opportunity to make something of his stewardship. If he had really feared the master so much, the very least he could have done was put the money in the bank, where it would be earning compound interest. The slave himself would still be guilty of avoiding his assignment, but at least the talent would be earning a minimal amount of interest. The wasted opportunity was therefore costly. Burying the talent was like stealing from the master. Even though the unfaithful servant did not embezzle money (like the unjust steward in Luke 16:1-12) or squander it in riotous living (like the prodigal son, Luke 15:13), his lack of diligence nonetheless cost his master money. It was morally tantamount to embezzlement or wanton extravagance.

Though he professed to fear the master, he had behaved in the most brazen and impudent manner—not only in squandering the opportunity he had been given, but also by trying to use his own day of reckoning as an occasion for such deliberate defamation of the master.

This sort of thing happens in real life all the time. People know very well that they have done wrong, but instead of humbly admitting their wrong, they concoct an accusation against the person to whom they are accountable. As the symbolism of the parable suggests, many even attempt this same vain tactic to try to justify themselves before God. They accuse Him of being too harsh or too demanding. I suppose many even think they can employ such a stratagem before the judgment throne. But it will not work. "Every mouth [will] be stopped, and all the world [will] become guilty before God" (Rom. 3:19). Like the wicked servant, the sinner will be condemned by his own words (Matt. 12:37).

The inconsistencies of the slave's rationalizing self-defense did not escape the master: "But his lord answered and said to him, 'You wicked and lazy servant, you knew that I reap where I have not sown, and gather where I have not scattered seed. So you ought to have deposited my money with the bankers, and at my coming I would have received back my own with interest'" (vv. 26-27). Ancient Rome had a banking system much like ours today. Deposits earned interest at about half the prime rate for loans. It wasn't much, but it would have been better than burying the money in the ground.

It is important to see that the master was not in any way conceding any truthfulness in the slave's accusations. He was merely pointing out that *if* there had been any truth whatsoever to the slave's complaint, it still did not explain the slave's behavior. He deliberately squandered every opportunity he had been given; but if the master's character had been as the slave portrayed, the slave's fear of the master would only have been more reason for him *not* to bury the talent in the ground. The slave was thus caught by his own wicked, slanderous lie.

The truth of the matter was that the slave had neither fear nor affection for his master. He was totally indifferent. He cared nothing for the master's interests, and that was made clear by his behavior. Contrast this wicked servant with the other two. The first two seized the opportunity to serve their master in his absence; the third man took advantage of the master's absence to pursue his own selfish ends. The first two were glad when the master returned, eager to see him, and ready to give an account; the third man was ashamed and guilty, and he responded by lashing out with a false accusation. The character of the men could hardly have been more different.

The third slave's sin lay not merely in the fact that he lost a profit. He might have worked hard and invested and still not done as well as the other two. He had less to work with than either of them anyway. But what really made his behavior galling was his utter disregard for his duty. He wasted opportunity. He never lifted a finger on behalf of his master. Had he honestly tried and lost money, it would have been less of a sin than his utter indifference and inactivity.

RECOMPENSE AND REWARD

The third slave was not merely unfaithful. He was faithless. He was loveless and disrespectful toward the master. His behavior showed a complete lack of concern about his master's business. His verbal attack showed a similar lack of any true or intimate knowledge of the master. The unfaithful servant clearly represents a professing Christian who is actually an unbeliever.

"Therefore take the talent from him, and give it to him who has ten talents. For to everyone who has, more will be given, and he will have abundance; but from him who does not have, even what he has will be taken away. And cast the unprofitable servant into the outer darkness. There will be weeping and gnashing of teeth."

—VV. 28-30

There's a stark and dramatic contrast between the reward for the faithful servants and the recompense given the unfaithful man. They heard the words, "Well done." He received a stern rebuke ("You wicked and lazy servant," v. 26). They were given increased responsibility. He was stripped of all he had. They were ushered into the joy of the Lord. He was cast into "outer darkness," an expression denoting hell, where there is "weeping and gnashing of teeth" (cf. Matt. 13:42, 50; 22:13; 24:51). Again our Lord departs from the temporal imagery of the parable and makes an explicit reference to hell in order to make the point and the symbolism of the parable clear: The wicked and lazy servant symbolizes the person cast into hell—all because of squandered opportunity.

Christ, the Master, is coming soon. Opportunity slips away with each passing minute. When He returns, it will be too late to recover lost opportunity. His judgment will occur immediately, and it will result in the final, irreversible disposition of all souls alive at His appearing—both faithful and unfaithful. Now is our only time to prepare. Today is the only opportunity we are guaranteed. All the resources we have belong to our Lord. Our opportunities for sharing the Gospel, our spiritual opportunities, and all temporal blessings come from His gracious hand. If these resources were ours, we could do with them as we please. But they are His, committed to us as His stewards, and we will give account at His coming for how we have used them.

Ten

The Judgment of the Sheep and Goats

Everything in the Olivet Discourse progresses toward a climactic judgment. Motifs of judgment involving the separation of believers from unbelievers run right through the discourse. We have seen already that all three of the parables in the discourse contain graphic symbols of coming judgment. And the great overriding theme of the whole discourse—the sudden appearing of Jesus Christ—is continually portrayed as the ultimate event that will precipitate and signal the arrival of a massive, catastrophic judgment. Now Christ gives a powerful description of that judgment:

> *"When the Son of Man comes in His glory, and all the holy angels with Him, then He will sit on the throne of His glory. All the nations will be gathered before Him, and He will separate them one from another, as a shepherd divides his sheep from the goats. And He will set the sheep on His right hand, but the goats on the left."*
>
> —MATT. 25:31-33

No one in Scripture had more to say about judgment than Jesus. He repeatedly warned about impending doom for the unrepentant (Luke 13:3, 5). He spoke of hell far more than of heaven and always in the most vivid and disturbing terms. Most of what we know about the everlasting doom of sinners came from the lips of the Savior. And none of the biblical descriptions of judgment are more severe or more intense than those given by Jesus.

Yet He always spoke of such things in the most tender and compassionate tones. He pleaded with sinners to turn from their sins, to be reconciled to God, and to take refuge in Him from the coming judgment. He better than anyone knew the high cost of sin and the severity of divine wrath against the sinner, for He would bear the full force of that wrath on behalf of those He redeemed. Therefore when He spoke of such things, He always spoke with the utmost empathy and not the least hostility. He even wept as he looked over Jerusalem, knowing that the city and the entire nation of Israel would reject Him as their Messiah and would soon suffer complete destruction.

> *He saw the city and wept over it, saying, "If you had known, even you, especially in this your day, the things that make for your peace! But now they are hidden from your eyes. For days will come upon you when your enemies will build an embankment around you, surround you and close you in on every side, and level you, and your children within you, to the ground; and they will not leave in you one stone upon another, because you did not know the time of your visitation."*
>
> —LUKE 19:41-44

In an important sense, the entire Olivet Discourse is simply an expansion of that compassionate plea. Beginning from the same starting point—a lament about the imminent destruction of Jerusalem—Christ simply broadens His perspective and gives the disciples an extended appeal that encompasses the whole eschatological future, right up to His return and the judgment that ensues. The same spirit that prompted Christ's weeping over the city of Jerusalem therefore permeates and colors the entire Olivet Discourse. And Matthew, who was there to hear it all firsthand, recorded it in His Gospel, where it stands as a beacon to all sinners throughout the entire age. It is the Lord's final tender plea for repentance before it is too late.

Looking back over the discourse, we see that all His various urgings to be faithful and all His admonitions to be prepared boil down to this: they are a compassionate call to repentance and faith in Him. He is warning us to be prepared for His coming because when He returns, He will bring final judgment. And as He concludes His discourse, He describes that judgment in detail.

This remaining part of the Olivet Discourse is one of the most severe and sobering warnings about judgment in all of Scripture. Christ the Great Shepherd is the Judge, and He separates His sheep from the goats. These words of Christ are not recorded in any of the other Gospels. But Matthew, intent on portraying Christ as King, here shows Him seated on His earthly throne. In fact, this judgment is His first act following His glorious return to earth, suggesting that judgment is His first order of business as *earthly* ruler (cf. Ps. 2:8-12). This event therefore inaugurates the millennial kingdom and is distinct from the Great White Throne judgment described in Revelation 20, which occurs *after* the millennial age is brought to a close. Here Christ is judging those alive at His coming, separating the sheep (true believers) from the goats (unbelievers). The goats represent the same class of people who are portrayed as evil servants, unwise virgins, and an unfaithful steward in the immediately preceding parables.

The Judge

Christ Himself is the Judge in the events described here. This is in keeping with what He said on another occasion: "For the Father judges no one, but has committed all judgment to the Son, that all should honor the Son just as they honor the Father" (John 5:22-23). Thus the same compassionate One who wept and pleaded with sinners to be reconciled to God will one day be their sovereign Judge.

And He will judge with "a rod of iron" (Rev. 19:15); He will "dash them to pieces like a potter's vessel" (Ps. 2:9; Rev. 2:27). The judgment will be fierce, pictured in Revelation 19:15 with the imagery of Christ "tread[ing] the winepress of the fierceness and wrath of Almighty God."

He will return with a large company of angels: "The Son of

Man comes in His glory, and all the holy angels with Him" (Matt. 25:31). Several passages of Scripture teach that the angels will play an assisting role in the judgment. According to 2 Thessalonians 1:7-8, "The Lord Jesus is revealed from heaven *with His mighty angels*, in flaming fire taking vengeance on those who do not know God, and on those who do not obey the gospel of our Lord Jesus Christ" (emphasis added). Matthew 24:31 says the angels will "gather together the elect from the four winds." Believers who have died or were caught up in the Rapture will also be part of the company that returns with Christ: "Behold, the Lord comes with ten thousands of His saints, to execute judgment on all" (Jude 14-15; cf. Zech. 14:5). "When Christ who is our life appears, then you also will appear with Him in glory" (Col. 3:4).

Here's an interesting fact: this passage in Matthew 25:31-46 marks the first time in any of Christ's recorded statements that He explicitly refers to Himself as King. Throughout His ministry He had much to say about the kingdom of God; but He did not expressly feature Himself as King until He did so in this context, speaking privately to the disciples. (Later, before Pilate, He publicly acknowledged that He is King—John 18:37.)

The title Christ most frequently applied to Himself was "Son of Man." Even here He employs that expression, but only to say that the Son of Man will come in His glory and subsequently take His *throne* (v. 31). In verse 34 he calls Himself "King" for the first time on record. Moreover, He declares that when He takes His rightful place as King, His first duty will be to execute righteous judgment, and thus to determine who will have the right to enter His kingdom.

THE TIME

Scripture is precise about the timing of this judgment. It will take place "when the Son of Man comes in His glory" (v. 31). Everything in the account suggests that His judgment will begin at the very moment He appears (cf. 24:30-41). This accords perfectly with the prophecy about His coming in Revelation 19:11-21:

> *Now I saw heaven opened, and behold, a white horse. And He who sat on him was called Faithful and True, and in righteousness He judges and makes war. His eyes were like a flame of fire, and on His head were many crowns. He had a name written that no one knew except Himself. He was clothed with a robe dipped in blood, and His name is called The Word of God. And the armies in heaven, clothed in fine linen, white and clean, followed Him on white horses. Now out of His mouth goes a sharp sword, that with it He should strike the nations. And He Himself will rule them with a rod of iron. He Himself treads the winepress of the fierceness and wrath of Almighty God. And He has on His robe and on His thigh a name written: KING OF KINGS AND LORD OF LORDS. Then I saw an angel standing in the sun; and he cried with a loud voice, saying to all the birds that fly in the midst of heaven, "Come and gather together for the supper of the great God, that you may eat the flesh of kings, the flesh of captains, the flesh of mighty men, the flesh of horses and of those who sit on them, and the flesh of all people, free and slave, both small and great." And I saw the beast, the kings of the earth, and their armies, gathered together to make war against Him who sat on the horse and against His army. Then the beast was captured, and with him the false prophet who worked signs in his presence, by which he deceived those who received the mark of the beast and those who worshiped his image. These two were cast alive into the lake of fire burning with brimstone. And the rest were killed with the sword which proceeded from the mouth of Him who sat on the horse. And all the birds were filled with their flesh.*

So when Christ appears, the opportunity for salvation will be gone forever. The day of mercy already spent, Christ will summarily cut off the wicked without remedy. Like the evil servant, they will be caught unawares by their Lord's return. Like the five foolish virgins, they will find the door closed and themselves locked out. Like the foolish and lazy steward, they will have no legitimate plea by which to excuse themselves. For them, the day of salvation is over.

Christ is returning to establish an earthly kingdom, and none but the sheep will be permitted to enter it.

THE PLACE

How do we know Christ will be seated on an *earthly* throne? Everything in the context points to this. He comes to earth in glory first; *"then* He will sit on the throne of His glory" (Matt. 25:31, emphasis added). This marks the establishment of the earthly kingdom, emanating from Jerusalem, that is spoken of so frequently in the Old Testament Messianic prophecies. This will be the fulfillment of the Davidic Covenant, given in 2 Samuel 7:12-16, 1 Chronicles 7:11-15, Psalm 89:3-4, and Zechariah 14:9. He will sit "upon the throne of David and over His kingdom, to order it and establish it with judgment and justice from that time forward, even forever" (Isa. 9:7). "He shall execute judgment and righteousness in the earth. In those days Judah will be saved, and Jerusalem will dwell safely" (Jer. 33:15-16). This signifies the fulfillment of the promise the angel gave Mary: "You will conceive in your womb and bring forth a Son, and shall call His name JESUS. He will be great, and will be called the Son of the Highest; and *the Lord God will give Him the throne of His father David.* And He will reign over the house of Jacob forever, and of His kingdom there will be no end" (Luke 1:31-33, emphasis added).

David's throne was an earthly one, in Jerusalem, and Scripture identifies Jerusalem as the place to which Christ will return, as well as the location of His throne:

> *In that day His feet will stand on the Mount of Olives, which faces Jerusalem on the east. And the Mount of Olives shall be split in two, from east to west, making a very large valley; half of the mountain shall move toward the north and half of it toward the south. . . . And in that day it shall be that living waters shall flow from*

Jerusalem, half of them toward the eastern sea and half of them toward the western sea; in both summer and winter it shall occur. And the LORD shall be King over all the earth. In that day it shall be—"The Lord is one," and His name one. All the land shall be turned into a plain from Geba to Rimmon south of Jerusalem. Jerusalem shall be raised up and inhabited in her place from Benjamin's Gate to the place of the First Gate and the Corner Gate, and from the Tower of Hananel to the king's winepresses. The people shall dwell in it; and no longer shall there be utter destruction, but Jerusalem shall be safely inhabited.

—ZECH. 14:4, 8-11

There is no good reason to interpret those promises in any sense except the literal one. Just as His ascension was literal and bodily, so shall He literally come in bodily form at His return. And since that is so, there is no valid reason to see His throne as anything but the literal reestablishment of David's earthly kingdom. His throne will be situated in Jerusalem, and Christ will rule over all the earth, finally bringing about the literal fulfillment of all the Old Testament millennial prophecies, as well as all the promises God made to Abraham about the land of Israel and all the promises He made to David about the throne.

But before the kingdom is established, a dreadful judgment must take place. Joel wrote of it centuries before Christ:

"Let the nations be wakened, and come up to the Valley of Jehoshaphat; for there I will sit to judge all the surrounding nations. Put in the sickle, for the harvest is ripe. Come, go down; for the winepress is full, the vats overflow—for their wickedness is great. Multitudes, multitudes in the valley of decision! For the day of the LORD is near in the valley of deci-sion. The sun and moon will grow dark, and the stars will diminish their brightness. The LORD also will roar from Zion, and utter His voice from Jerusalem; the heavens and earth will shake; but the LORD will be a shelter for His people, and the strength of the children of Israel. So you shall know that I am the LORD your God, dwelling in Zion

My holy mountain. Then Jerusalem shall be holy, and no aliens shall
ever pass through her again."

—JOEL 3:12-17

Thus God Himself pledged that the sheep would be separated
from the goats. And none but those who love Christ will be permitted to enter or pass through His kingdom.

THE SUBJECTS

Some suggest that the subjects of this judgment are political entities—literal nations. After all, Matthew 25:32 says, "All the nations
will be gathered before Him, and He will separate them one from
another." (The passage cited above from Joel also speaks to
"nations.")

But the Greek term translated "nations" in Matthew 25:32 is
ethna (from which we derive our word *ethnic*), and it speaks of *peo-*
ples, not political or national entities. Furthermore, the context
makes clear that individuals are in view in this judgment:

"Then the King will say to those on His right hand, 'Come, you
blessed of My Father, inherit the kingdom prepared for you from the
foundation of the world: for I was hungry and you gave Me food; I
was thirsty and you gave Me drink; I was a stranger and you took
Me in; I was naked and you clothed Me; I was sick and you visited
Me; I was in prison and you came to Me.' Then the righteous will
answer Him, saying, 'Lord, when did we see You hungry and feed
You, or thirsty and give You drink? When did we see You a stranger
and take You in, or naked and clothe You? Or when did we see You
sick, or in prison, and come to You?' And the King will answer and
say to them, 'Assuredly, I say to you, inasmuch as you did it to one
of the least of these My brethren, you did it to Me.' Then He will
also say to those on the left hand, 'Depart from Me, you cursed, into
the everlasting fire prepared for the devil and his angels: for I was
hungry and you gave Me no food; I was thirsty and you gave Me no
drink; I was a stranger and you did not take Me in, naked and you

*did not clothe Me, sick and in prison and you did not visit Me.'
Then they also will answer Him, saying, 'Lord, when did we see
You hungry or thirsty or a stranger or naked or sick or in prison, and
did not minister to You?' Then He will answer them, saying,
'Assuredly, I say to you, inasmuch as you did not do it to one of the
least of these, you did not do it to Me.' And these will go away into
everlasting punishment, but the righteous into eternal life."*

—VV. 34-46

That describes a judgment based on actions for which people are individually responsible. The punishment also applies to individuals, not corporate groups. The notion that political entities could be the subjects of this judgment is completely foreign to the text.

THE PROCESS

The focus and goal of this judgment is the separation of the righteous from the unrighteous. By this judgment is brought to pass what Christ prophesied earlier in the discourse when He said, "Two men will be in the field: one will be taken and the other left. Two women will be grinding at the mill: one will be taken and the other left" (24:40-41). This judgment also fulfills what was represented by the closing of the banquet door to the foolish virgins.

Notice that the judgment is not designed for Christ to *discover* who are sheep and who are goats; He knows this at the start of the judgment, when He seats the sheep on the right hand (the place of favor) and the goats on the left (the place of disfavor) (25:33). "The Lord [already] knows those who are His" (2 Tim. 2:19). "He calls his own sheep by name and leads them out" (John 10:3). The purpose of the judgment is therefore only to render a formal verdict between the sheep and the goats.

The significance of the sheep-and-goat imagery would have been obvious to the disciples. They were familiar with the sight of sheep and goats being herded together. (The same practice can be observed in the Middle East today.) A single shepherd can easily oversee both kinds of creatures together, but the character of the two animals are markedly different. Sheep are docile, gentle creatures. Goats are often unruly and hyperactive. So the two cannot easily be kept in the same fold at night. A shepherd would therefore separate the animals in the evening before closing them in pens.

The Great Shepherd will undertake a similar process before the launch of His millennial kingdom. The believing sheep will be welcomed into their domain—a kingdom full of blessings that will never end. And the unbelieving goats will be sent to a place of punishment that will never end.

THE EVIDENCE

Jesus as Judge cites the evidence that proves who is fit for the kingdom and who is not. It is the testimony of what they thought of Jesus, as evidenced by how they have treated His brethren.

Many imagine support for a doctrine of salvation by works in Jesus' words to the faithful. But the context clearly rules out such an interpretation, because our Lord makes clear that their destiny was settled and the kingdom prepared for them by the gracious decree of a sovereign God "from the foundation of the world" (Matt. 25:34). In other words, their inheritance was settled in eternity past, long ages before they had done any good or evil, "[so] that the purpose of God according to election might stand, not of works but of Him who calls" (Rom. 9:11).

So the words of Christ underscore the biblical truth of divine election. The sheep are sheep by the grace of God alone, not because of anything they have done to make themselves worthy.

Yet their deeds are clear *evidence* of their election. These deeds are the fruit of faith. And therefore works are fitting evidence to be cited either for or against people in judgment (cf. Rom. 2:5-10). Christ is in effect saying, "You are the chosen children of My Father, and your faith is made clear by the service you have rendered to Me. Welcome into My kingdom" (v. 40).

The works He cites involve compassion shown to His people

by ministering to them when they are hungry, thirsty, alienated, naked, sick, or imprisoned. Such good deeds are "pure and unde-filed religion," the truest evidence of a vibrant, living faith (Jas. 1:27). The one who lacks such deeds reveals "dead" faith, not the living kind (cf. Jas. 2:15-17). The apostle John said something sim-ilar: "Whoever has this world's goods, and sees his brother in need, and shuts up his heart from him, how does the love of God abide in him? My little children, let us not love in word or in tongue, but in deed and in truth" (1 John 3:17-18).

So Christ is not suggesting that such good works are *meritorious* for salvation. But they are vital evidence that the principle of eter-nal life really exists within a person.

Notice that those who receive the King's commendation are surprised (Matt. 25:37-39). They seem almost unaware that their deeds constituted service to Christ. Much less were they thinking they might have earned his favor by such works. The good deeds were merely the natural outflow of a heart of faith.

THE CONDEMNATION

The goats are consigned to eternal punishment on similar grounds. They have proved by their works that they are "cursed" (v. 41). Christ no more condemns these people solely because they failed to do good works than He saves the others because of their works. The goats are accursed because they are wicked unbeliev-ers. Their unfitness for the kingdom stems from a constitutional sinfulness, not merely from a shortage of philanthropic good works. They despise the King, and their contempt for Him is clearly displayed in their treatment of His people. These are Christ-rejecting unbelievers, not merely people who failed to be altruistic enough.

They are as surprised as the righteous ones were about Christ's verdict. They protest that they have not consciously or deliberately slighted Christ, but Christ exposes their guilt by calling to mind their treatment of His people—or rather their total indifference (vv.

44-45). His words of condemnation to them are an exact but inverted echo of His earlier commendation of the righteous.

The goats are eternally separated from all that is good and righteous, and they are consigned forever to "the everlasting fire prepared for the devil and his angels" (v. 41). Christ describes hell as a place of "everlasting punishment" (v. 46) from which there is no relief or respite forever. The English translation of this verse speaks of "everlasting punishment" and "eternal life," but in the Greek text the same word is used for both "everlasting" and "eternal." It is the word *aiōnios*, which denotes something perpetual, something never-ending. The double use of the word establishes a deliberate parallel. Christ thereby signifies that the punishment of the wicked is eternal in the same sense as the reward of the righteous. This verse therefore overturns the view of those who believe the wicked will simply be eradicated from existence. Here and throughout Scripture we are taught that the torment of hell is as endless and unremitting as the blessedness of heaven (cf. v. 41; Dan. 12:2; Mark 9:43-48; Luke 16:22-26; 2 Thess. 1:9; Rev. 14:11; 20:10).

The millennial kingdom will cover the entire earth; so those excluded will not even be permitted to remain alive on earth. "They will *go away* into everlasting punishment" (emphasis added).

The righteous, however, are admitted to "eternal life." They will enter the kingdom in an unglorified state and then be glorified at the end of the thousand years.[1] Their admission to the millennial kingdom is the threshold of eternal life for them. Although they enter the kingdom in an unglorified state, there is no reason to assume they will subsequently die. With the earth under the rule of righteousness, the human life span will be restored to the antediluvian norm—and probably even longer (cf. Isa. 65:20). All those who enter the kingdom could therefore survive the whole thousand years, after which they will be glorified and enter fully into the eternal state. Thus entering the kingdom, they are said to enter "into eternal life."

The future of the unrighteous and the future of the righteous could hardly be more starkly different. The implication of this is plain: the time to think deeply about one's destiny is now. The time to prepare for judgment is now. The day of salvation is now. And those who wait until Christ returns will find it is already too late. We don't know the day or the hour of His return. But the time is fast approaching.

It's time to get ready.

"Watch therefore, for you do not know when the master of the house is coming—in the evening, at midnight, at the crowing of the rooster, or in the morning—lest, coming suddenly, he find you sleeping. And what I say to you, I say to all: Watch!"

—MARK 13:35-37

Epilogue

HOW TO PREPARE
FOR
CHRIST'S RETURN

*D*ear reader, if you are uncertain of how to prepare your heart and life for Christ's return, this brief epilogue is for you. As we noted in the book, the only appropriate preparedness for Christ's coming is a *spiritual* preparation. Neither religious ceremony nor mere behavioral reform can possibly prepare you to meet Him. Even if you were able to live a perfect life from now on, you must still face judgment for your past misdeeds. So true readiness for Christ's return must include an assurance that your past guilt is forgiven and that your present standing before God is secure. Fortunately, Scripture clearly reveals how we can have such an assurance.

HOW WE CAN KNOW OUR SINS ARE FORGIVEN

Scripture teaches that even one failure to meet the absolutely perfect standard of God's law is enough sin to condemn you eternally. "For whoever shall keep the whole law, and yet stumble in one point, he is guilty of all" (Jas. 2:10). But the truth is, all of us are guilty of multiple failures. "There is none righteous, no, not one" (Rom. 3:10). "All have sinned and fall short of the glory of God" (v. 23).

An atonement is needed for our sins. But expiating our own sins is not something we can do. The price of sin is too high. "For the wages of sin is death" (Rom. 6:23). Good works can never atone for evil works. "The soul who sins shall die" (Ezek. 18:20). Nothing we can do, short of eternal punishment, could possibly render justice for our evil deeds. The price of sin is unimaginably high. It is infinitely more than we can bear. "Without shedding of blood there is no remission" (Heb. 9:22).

But Christ made atonement for our sins by shedding His blood, dying for us. He bore the guilt of those who trust Him, and He suffered on their behalf the price of their sins. What they could not bear, He bore on their behalf, suffering the most humiliating and agonizing death imaginable.

> *Surely He has borne our griefs and carried our sorrows; yet we esteemed Him stricken, smitten by God, and afflicted. But He was wounded for our transgressions, He was bruised for our iniquities; the chastisement for our peace was upon Him, and by His stripes we are healed. All we like sheep have gone astray; we have turned, every one, to his own way; and the LORD has laid on Him the iniquity of us all*
> —ISA. 53:4-6

> *[God] made Him who knew no sin to be sin for us, that we might become the righteousness of God in Him.*
> —2 COR. 5:21

He shed His own innocent blood as an atonement for the sins of others. No lesser sacrifice could have met the demands of justice for our sins, "for it is the blood that makes atonement for the soul" (Lev. 17:11). And God was pleased by His Son's sacrifice (Isa. 53:10). Christ rose from the dead to signify His triumph (Rom. 1:4).

He now freely offers forgiveness to all who will trust Christ. No merit of our own is necessary to earn forgiveness. Christ has purchased full pardon on behalf of all who will simply lay hold of it by faith. He has already done all the work of atonement and redemption for His people (Eph. 1:7; Col. 1:14). "Therefore we conclude that a man is justified by faith apart from the deeds of the law" (Rom. 3:28).

That's why the Gospel is "good news." The work of our salvation is something God Himself does on our behalf. We simply lay hold of redemption by faith.

HOW WE CAN SECURE A RIGHT STANDING BEFORE GOD

But there's more to Christ's redeeming work than just forgiveness for our past sins. He also provides us a righteous standing before God. If all our sins were forgiven and the slate wiped clean (but nothing more), all we would have is a blank slate. But believers in Christ receive far more than a blank slate. Righteousness is imputed to them. It is a righteousness that they have not earned for themselves by any means; it is credited to their account by faith alone.

> *To him who does not work but believes on Him who justifies the ungodly, his faith is accounted for righteousness, just as David also describes the blessedness of the man to whom God imputes righteousness apart from works: "Blessed are those whose lawless deeds are forgiven, and whose sins are covered; blessed is the man to whom the LORD shall not impute sin."*
>
> —ROM. 4:5-8

Saul of Tarsus hoped his own religious deeds would earn him enough righteousness to be acceptable to God. But Christ met him on the Damascus Road and transformed the proud Pharisee into Paul the apostle. Paul therefore renounced his own works as "rubbish" (Phil. 3:4-8) and instead placed all his hope in a righteousness that was not his own. Rather than seeking to *earn* a right standing with God, Paul's only hope from then on was to "gain Christ and be found in Him, not having my own righteousness, which is from the law, but that which is through faith in Christ, the righteousness which is from God by faith" (vv. 8-9).

He was speaking of the righteousness that is imputed to everyone who trusts Christ alone for salvation. It is the perfect righteousness of Christ Himself, imputed to everyone who believes (cf.

Gen. 15:6). That righteousness is the only ground on which we can stand with confidence before God. If you have not embraced Christ as your sole hope of salvation, I urge you to do so even now.

> . . . *as though God were pleading through us: we implore you on Christ's behalf, be reconciled to God.*
>
> —2 COR 5:20

WHAT WE MUST DO WHILE WE WAIT FOR CHRIST

If you are certain about your reconciliation with God, that is a wonderful assurance. But there's more to do while we await His coming. We can sum it up with this: stay busy *serving Him* until He comes. That was the whole lesson of the parable of the talents. It was also a major thrust of all Jesus' instructions about readiness. What activities should occupy us while we wait? Scripture suggests several.

Worship. "The hour is coming, and now is, when the true worshipers will worship the Father in spirit and truth; for the Father is seeking such to worship Him" (John 4:23). Worship should permeate our whole lives, so that we seek to do everything, including our eating and drinking, to the glory of God (1 Cor. 10:31). But corporate worship also plays a necessary and distinctive role in the life of the Christian. Gathering with God's people to worship Him is something we must not neglect while we await Christ's coming.

Fellowship and encouragement. "Let us consider one another in order to stir up love and good works, not forsaking the assembling of ourselves together, as is the manner of some, but exhorting one another, and so much the more as you see the Day approaching" (Hebrews 10:24-25). Christian fellowship is also vital for its steadying influence as we exhort and encourage one another. For all these reasons, every Christian should make a habit of regular, faithful involvement and membership in a local church. If you have come to Christ for the first time while reading this book, I urge you to seek fellowship with like-minded believers in the context of a church where Scripture is believed and taught.

Evangelism and discipleship. "Go therefore and make disciples of all the nations, baptizing them in the name of the Father and of the Son and of the Holy Spirit, teaching them to observe all things that I have commanded you; and lo, I am with you always, even to the end of the age" (Matt. 28:19-20). That is our Lord's Great Commission, His final instructions to His disciples before He ascended into heaven. Those are our marching orders. It is the main business we are to be about while we await His return.

Prayer. "Praying always with all prayer and supplication in the Spirit, being watchful to this end with all perseverance and supplication for all the saints" (Eph. 6:18). Prayer is like breathing to the Christian. It is absolutely necessary to our spiritual vitality. It is the crucial spiritual link we have with Christ while we await His return. Therefore, a vigorous prayer life is one of the best ways to keep from becoming languid and indifferent while He tarries.

Bible study. "Be diligent to present yourself approved to God, a worker who does not need to be ashamed, rightly dividing the word of truth" (2 Tim. 2:15). If prayer is like spiritual breathing, Scripture is our spiritual food. "As newborn babes, desire the pure milk of the word, that you may grow thereby" (1 Pet. 2:2). If we don't want to be ashamed at His coming, we need to study to be His approved workers by learning to understand His Word rightly.

Ministry to others. "Whoever has this world's goods, and sees his brother in need, and shuts up his heart from him, how does the love of God abide in him? My little children, let us not love in word or in tongue, but in deed and in truth" (1 John 3:17-18). Taking a clue from our Lord's words about the sheep-and-goats judgment, we know there is much practical work to be done while we wait for Christ. Many are needy and disconsolate. We have means to meet both physical and spiritual needs, and we are called to meet as many such needs as we can.

Only if we stay busy in all these ways while we wait for Him can we expect to hear Him say, "Well done."

Appendix

THE IMMINENT RETURN OF THE REDEEMER

By Arthur W. Pink[1]

Nowhere in the Bible is the actual time of the Second Advent made known; instead, it is presented as an event that may occur at *any* hour. Or, in other words, the fact of the Savior's appearing is invariably set forth *in the language of imminency*. When we say that the Redeemer's return is an imminent event, we do not mean it will occur *immediately*, but that He *may* come back in our lifetime, that He *may* come back this year. Yet we cannot say that He *will* do so.

The *fact* of the Second Advent is certain because it is expressly revealed in Holy Writ. The *date* of the Second Advent is *uncertain* because it has not been made known by God. Here then we have a truth that is simple to grasp, yet one that is of fundamental importance and great practical value. The majority of the errors and heresies that have gathered around this subject are directly traceable to the ignoring of this elementary consideration.

For example: if the Lord's people had given due heed to the fact that Scripture presents the Second Coming of Christ as something that may happen *at any hour*, then the postmillennial teaching that our Lord will not come back again for more than a thousand years would never have obtained the hearing and acceptance that it has received. Furthermore, if the wondrous truth that our Redeemer might return *today* once took firm hold on our hearts, it would revolutionize our lives and provide us with a spiritual dynamic that is incalculable in its reach and incomparable in its value. Without expatiating any further upon the general bearings of this aspect of our theme, let us now proceed to show that—

OUR LORD HIMSELF SPOKE OF HIS RETURN IN THE LANGUAGE OF IMMINENCY

In the Olivet Discourse, where the Master replied to the inquiries of His disciples concerning the sign of His coming and of the end of the age, He said—

> *Watch therefore;* for ye know not what hour your Lord doth come. *But know this, that if the goodman of the house had known in what watch the thief would come, he would have watched, and would not have suffered his house to be broken up. Therefore be ye also ready:* for in such an hour as ye think not the Son of man cometh. *Who then is a faithful and wise servant, whom his lord hath made ruler over his household, to give them meat in due season? Blessed is that servant, whom his lord when he cometh shall find so doing. Verily I say unto you, That he shall make him ruler over all his goods. But and if that evil servant shall say in his heart, My lord delayeth his coming; and shall begin to smite his fel-lowservants, and to eat and drink with the drunken; the lord of that servant shall come in a day when he looketh not for him, and in an hour that he is not aware of, and shall cut him asunder, and appoint him his portion with the hypocrites: there shall be weeping and gnashing of teeth.*
>
> —MATT. 24:42-51[2]

An analysis of the above passage reveals the following important truths. First, the "hour" of our Lord's return is *unknown* to His people. Second, because we know not the exact time of His appearing, we must be in an attitude of *constant* expectation and watchfulness. Third, the Lord *will* return *unexpectedly,* even in such an hour as His own people "think not." Fourth, the faithful and wise servant is he who shall give meat in due season to those of the Lord's household during the time of Christ's absence, and the one who is found so occupied at the time of His appearing shall be richly rewarded. Fifth, the one who shall say in his heart, "My Lord *delayeth* His coming" is an *"evil* servant," and such a one shall receive a portion of shame at our Lord's return.

The parable of the ten virgins intimates that the Lord Jesus desired His people to maintain an attitude of constant readiness for the appearing of the Bridegroom. At the beginning of the parable He pictures all of the "virgins" taking their lamps and going forth to "meet" Him. The interpretation of this part of the parable is very simple. In the early days after our Lord's departure from the earth, His followers detached themselves from all worldly interests and set their affections on Christ—His return being their one hope and great desire. But when the Bridegroom tarried, the expectation of His appearing disappeared, and spiritual sloth and sleep was the inevitable consequence, and this condition prevailed until the midnight cry arose—"Behold, the Bridegroom cometh; go ye out to meet him." The effect of this cry is seen in the arousing of both the wise and the foolish virgins. The need of preparation and watchfulness is disclosed in the doom that overtook those who had no oil in their vessels. The practical application of the whole parable was made by the Lord Himself—"Watch therefore; *for ye know neither the day nor the hour wherein the Son of Man cometh*" (25:13).

At the close of Mark's account of the Olivet Discourse he records at greater length than does Matthew our Lord's command to His disciples to *watch* for His return—"Take ye heed, watch and pray: for ye know not when the time is. For the Son of man is as a man taking a far journey, who left his house, and gave authority to his servants, and to every man his work, and commanded the porter to watch. Watch ye therefore: *for ye know not when the Master of the house cometh*, at even, or at midnight, or at the cockcrowing, or in the morning: lest coming suddenly he find you sleeping. And what I say unto you I say unto all, Watch" (Mark 13:33-37). A careful reading of these verses makes it apparent that the design of the Master was to impress upon His disciples two things: First, that while it was certain He *would* return, yet it was uncertain *when* He would appear; second, that in view of the uncertainty of the exact hour of His second coming, the Lord's followers must maintain an attitude of constant watchfulness, looking for Him to return *at any moment.*

On another occasion the Lord said to His disciples:

> *Let your loins be girded about, and your lights burning; and ye yourselves like unto men* that wait for their Lord, *when he will return from the wedding; that, when he cometh and knocketh, they may open unto him immediately. Blessed are those servants, whom the Lord when he cometh shall find watching: verily I say unto you, that he shall gird himself, and make them to sit down to meat, and will come forth and serve them. And if he shall come in the second watch, or come in the third watch, and find them so, blessed are those servants.*
>
> —LUKE 12:35-38

The comparison is a very impressive one. The believer is exhorted to be like a faithful servant, standing on the threshold with loins girded and his lamp lighted, peering through the darkness for the first sight of his returning Master and listening eagerly with attentive ear for the first sounds of His approaching steps.

> *Even thus shall it be in the day when the Son of man is revealed. In that day, he which shall be upon the housetop, and his stuff in the house, let him not come down to take it away: and he that is in the field, let him likewise not return back. . . . I tell you, in that night there shall be two men in one bed; the one shall be taken, and the other shall be left. Two women shall be grinding together; the one shall be taken, and the other left.*
>
> —LUKE 17:30-35

The force of this passage is in full harmony with the others already considered. The Lord's appearing is to be unannounced and unexpected. It will occur while men are busy at their daily vocations, and therefore it behooves us to be constantly on the *qui vive.*[3] In passing, we may observe how the last quoted Scripture brings out the marvelous *scientific accuracy* of the Bible. We are told in verse 31 above that it shall be "day" (in one part of the earth) at the time Christ is "revealed" (v. 30), while in verse 34 we learn it will be "night" (in another part of the earth), thus anticipating a comparatively recent discovery of science and demonstrating that the Lord Jesus was perfectly cognizant of the *rotundity* and *rotation* of the earth!

> *And take heed to yourselves,* lest at any time *your hearts be overcharged with surfeiting, and drunkenness, and cares of this life, and so that day come upon you* unawares. *For as a snare shall it come on all them that dwell on the face of the whole earth.* Watch *ye therefore, and pray always, that ye may be accounted worthy to escape all these things that shall come to pass, and to stand before the Son of man.*
>
> —LUKE 21:34-36

Mark particularly, above, the words "lest at any time your hearts be overcharged with surfeiting [self-indulgence] . . . and so that day come upon you unawares." Daily—nay, *hourly*—readiness is required of us. Language could not be more explicit. Let those who speak so disparagingly of the "any moment theory" weigh the words "at any time" and remember they were uttered by the Lord Himself. The precise date of the Second Advent has been designedly withheld from us in order that we should maintain our attitude of watchfulness and that we remain on the very tiptoe of expectation.

One verse of Scripture needs to be noted in this connection ere we turn to our next point. It has often been objected by postmillennialists that in view of our Lord's declaration, "This gospel of the kingdom shall be preached in all the world for a witness unto all nations; and then shall the end come" (Matt. 24:14), it was *impossible* for the apostles to be expecting Christ to *return in their own lifetime.* But this objection is disposed of by several passages recorded in the New Testament itself. In Acts 19:10 we read, "And this continued by the space of two years; so that *all they which dwelt in Asia* heard the word of the Lord Jesus, both Jews and Greeks." And again, in Colossians 1:5-6 we are told, "for the hope which is laid up for you in heaven, whereof ye heard before in the word of the truth of the gospel; which is come unto you, *as it is in all the world*," and in verse 23 of the same chapter, "be not moved away from the hope of the gospel, which ye have heard, and which was preached *to every creature which is under heaven*; whereof I Paul am made a minister." From these passages then it is abundantly clear that no such formidable hindrance as imagined by postmillennialists interposed between the apostles and the hope of the imminent return of the Redeemer. Scripture thus affords positive evidence that the Gospel *had been* so widely diffused by the apostles themselves that nothing further *necessarily* and *inevitably* intervened between them and the realization of their hope.

Having thus, we trust, satisfactorily disposed of the most plausible and forcible objection which can be brought against the premillennial and imminent return of our Lord, let us now consider—

THE APOSTLES REFERRED TO THE REDEEMER'S RETURN IN THE LANGUAGE OF IMMINENCY

"Knowing the time, that now it is high time to awake out of sleep: for now is our salvation nearer than when we believed. The night is far spent, *the day is at hand*: let us therefore cast off the works of darkness, and let us put on the armor of light" (Rom. 13:11-12). The "salvation" to which the apostle here refers is the completing and consummating of our salvation, when we shall in spirit and soul and body be fully conformed to the image of God's Son. The time when this will be realized is the time of our Redeemer's return, for "when he shall appear, *we shall be like him*" (1 John 3:2). That time will be the believer's "day," that "perfect day" unto which the path of the just "shineth more and more" (Prov. 4:18). The "night," spoken of above, is the present period during which the Light of the world is absent. Observe that the apostle, under the Holy Spirit, regarded the night as "far spent," and the day as "at hand."

"And the God of peace shall bruise Satan under your feet *shortly*" (Rom. 16:20). The reference here is to Genesis 3:15, where we have recorded Jehovah's promise to our first parents that the woman's Seed would bruise the head of the Serpent. As believers will, in the coming day, rule and reign with Christ (Rev. 3:21, 19:14; 20:4), it is here said, "The God of peace shall bruise Satan under *your* feet." Concerning the use of the word "shortly," the apostle did not regard the fulfillment of this promise as something that lay in the far distant future, but rather as that which was even then impending.

"I thank my God always on your behalf, for the grace of God which is given you by Jesus Christ; that in everything ye are enriched by him, in all utterance, and in all knowledge; even as the testimony of Christ was confirmed in you: so that ye come behind in no gift; *waiting for the coming of our Lord Jesus Christ*" (1 Cor. 1:4-7). From this passage we learn, first, that these Corinthian saints were "waiting" for the coming of the Lord Jesus, which proved they were looking for Him to return *in their generation*; second, that the apostle *commended* them for their attitude, yea, "thank[ed] God always on [their] behalf"; third, that this expectation on the part of these Corinthian believers was the very *summum bonum* of Christian experience, inasmuch as it is said, "ye come behind in no gift," and then as a climax it is added, "waiting for the coming of our Lord Jesus Christ."

"Let us consider one another to provoke unto love and to good works: not forsaking the assembling of ourselves together, as the manner of some is; but exhorting one another: and so much the more, *as ye see the day approaching*" (Heb. 10:24-25). The coming "day" with its glories and blessedness was that which filled the apostle's vision. The promised "day," the Day of Christ, which was to follow this dark night of sorrow when the Bridegroom is absent, was the hope that established his heart. He could "see," by faith, that Day *approaching*, and on the fact of its *imminency* he bases an exhortation to those who are partakers of the heavenly calling to conduct themselves in the present in a manner befitting those who are the children of light. Again in this same chapter the apostle says, "*For yet a little while*, and he that shall come will come, and will not tarry" (v.

37). How clear it is from these words that the Holy Spirit desired the first-century believers to be *"looking for* that blessed hope, and the glorious appearing of the great God and our Saviour Jesus Christ"!

So real was the hope of the Redeemer's return to the heart of the apostle Paul and so imminent did this event appear to him that we find *he included himself* among those who might not fall asleep but be among the living saints when the assembling shout should be heard. Said he, "Behold, I show you a mystery; *we* shall not all sleep, but *we* shall all be changed in a moment, in the twinkling of an eye" (1 Cor. 15:51-52). Again, "For *our* conversation is in heaven; from whence also *we* look for the Saviour, the Lord Jesus Christ: who shall change *our* vile body, that it may be fashioned like unto his glorious body" (Phil. 3:20-21). Once more, "For the Lord himself shall descend from heaven with a shout, with the voice of the archangel, and with the trump of God: and the dead in Christ shall rise first: then *we* which are alive and remain shall be caught up together with them in the clouds, to meet the Lord in the air: and so shall *we* ever be with the Lord" (1 Thess. 4:16-17). The enemies of the faith have seized upon these very statements to show that the apostle Paul was in error, that he wrote by unaided human wisdom, that he merely recorded in his epistles *his own beliefs*, and that in some of these he was clearly mistaken. But such an objection is quite pointless to the saints who believe that *"All* Scripture is given by inspiration of God." We hope to show further on in this chapter *why* the Holy Spirit moved the apostles to write of the Second Advent of Christ as an event that might take place in their own day.

The apostle Paul was not alone in this regard: we find that the other apostles also regarded the return of our Lord as something that might occur at any time. The apostle James wrote, "Be ye also patient; stablish your hearts: for the coming of the Lord draweth nigh" (Jas. 5:8). There is no ambiguity about this language: such a statement not only argued the premillennial coming of Christ, inasmuch as His coming could not have been said to "draw nigh" if a whole millennium intervened, but it also announced the *imminency* of His return—something that might be expected at any time. The apostle Peter declared, "But the end of all things [all things connected with this present regime] *is at hand:* be ye therefore sober, and watch unto prayer" (1 Pet. 4:7). The apostle was expecting the speedy winding up of this present economy and the introduction of a new order of things when his Lord returned and took the government upon His shoulder. The apostle John said, "Little children, it is *the last time*: and as ye have heard that antichrist shall come, even now are there many antichrists; whereby we know that it is the last time" (1 John 2:18). The force of the apostle's statement was to the effect that though the personal Antichrist had not appeared up to the time when he wrote his epistle, yet the saints must not conclude from this that the Second Coming of Christ was necessarily a long way off. No, for even then there were many antichrists, by which they were to know it was "the last time." Thus we see that the testimony of the apostles was uniform and explicit. They were looking for their Lord to return at any time. Such ought to be our attitude too.

> *Let not my eyes with tears be dim,*
> *Let joy their upward glance illume;*
> *Look up, and watch, and wait for Him—*
> *Soon, soon the Lord will come.*
>
> *Soon will that star-paved Milky Way,*
> *Soon will that beauteous azure dome,*
> *Glories, ne'er yet conceived display—*
> *Soon, soon the Lord will come.*
>
> *Changed in the twinkling of an eye,*
> *Invested with immortal bloom,*
> *I shall behold Him throned on high,*
> *And sing, "The Lord is come!"*
>
> *One beam from His all-glorious face*
> *These mortal garments will consume,*
> *Each sinful blemish will efface—*
> *Lord Jesus, quickly come!*

What will it be with Thee to dwell,
Thyself my everlasting Home!
Oh, bliss—Oh, joy ineffable!
Lord Jesus, quickly come!

WHY WAS THE FACT OF OUR LORD'S RETURN PRESENTED IN THE LANGUAGE OF IMMINENCY BUT THE EXACT DATE WITHHELD?

At first sight it may appear strange that our Lord has not made known to us the precise date of His appearing. He has caused many details concerning the Blessed Hope to be recorded in the Word. He has made known many things that are to transpire at His Second Advent, and in view of the fact that so much *has been* revealed it may strike us as peculiar that the very point upon which human curiosity most desires enlightenment should have been left undefined. We need hardly say that it was *not ignorance* on our Lord's part that caused Him to leave the hour of His Second Coming undetermined, though some of His enemies have dared to charge this against Him, basing their evil indictment upon Mark 13:32—"But of that day and that hour knoweth no man, no, not the angels which are in heaven, neither the Son, but the Father." These words need occasion no difficulty if we pay due attention to the particular Gospel in which they are found, namely, Mark's—the Gospel of the Servant of Jehovah. The purpose of Mark's Gospel is to present the Lord Jesus as the perfect Servant, the obedient Servant, the Servant whose meat it was to do the will of Him who sent Him; and "the servant knoweth not what his lord doeth" (John 15:15). Mark 13:32 does not call into question our Lord's omniscience but asserts that, as a Servant, He waited upon Another's will. A little reflection will reveal the perfect wisdom of our Lord in concealing the exact date of His return. One reason was that He desired to keep His people on the very tiptoe of expectation, continually looking for Him.

Again, this question needs to be pondered in the light of *the unity of Christ's church*. The tendency with all of us is to regard believers as so many detached individuals, instead of viewing the saints as "one body" (1 Cor. 12:13), "members one of another" (Rom. 12:5). The church is not an organization; it is a living organism, a "body" of which Christ is the "head." Hence, the imminency of the Redeemer's return is to one member precisely what it is to *all* the members, and therefore first-century believers were just as truly interested in the appearing of the Savior as the believers now living in the twentieth century. The object of hope then is the object of hope now, for the Body is one; and conversely, the object of hope now must necessarily have been the object of hope then. Consequently, the early Christians, by virtue of the unity of the saints, were exhorted to walk in the light of the blessing of a hope that is *common to the entire church*.

The return of our Lord might not have been revealed at all, but in that case a most powerful dynamic to godly living would have been withheld from the church. The imminency of the Redeemer's Second Advent was revealed as an incentive to watchfulness and preparedness. If then the fact of our Lord's return had not been presented in the New Testament as something that *might* occur at any time, but instead had been expressly postponed and fixed to happen in some particular and distant century, then all believers who lived in the centuries preceding that one would have been robbed of the comfort that is to be found in the assurance that Christ may return at any hour and would have lost the purifying effects that such a prospect is calculated to produce. As it has been well remarked, "It is not that He desires each succeeding generation to believe that He will certainly return in their time, for He does not desire our faith and our practice to be founded on error, as, in that case, the faith and practice of all generations except the last would be. But it is a necessary element of the doctrine concerning [the Second Coming of Christ] that it should be possible at any time, that no generation should consider it improbable as theirs" (Archbishop Trench).

Here then is the simple but sufficient answer to our question. The Second Coming of Christ is presented in the language of imminency because of the far-reaching effects it is designed to exert on those who lay hold of the promise, "Behold, I come quickly." The imminent return of the Redeemer is a *practical* hope. It is the commanding motive of the New Testament. The Holy Spirit has linked it with every precept and practice of Christian character and conduct. As another has so well expressed it: "It arms admonitions, it points appeals, it strengthens arguments, it enforces commands, it intensifies entreaties, it arouses courage, it rebukes fear, it quickens affection, it kindles hope, it inflames zeal, it separates from the world, it consecrates to God, it dries tears, it conquers death" (Brookes). To amplify this statement in detail—

The hope of our Lord's Second Coming produces *loyalty and faithfulness to Christ*.

> *Who then is that faithful and wise steward, whom his lord shall make ruler over his household, to give them their portion of meat in due season? Blessed is that servant, whom his lord when he cometh shall find so doing. Of a truth I say unto you, that he will make him ruler over all that he hath. But and if that servant say in his heart, My lord delayeth his coming; and shall begin to beat the menservants and maidens, and to eat and drink, and to be drunken; the lord of that servant will come in a day when he looketh not for him, and at an hour when he is not aware, and will cut him in sunder, and will appoint him his portion with the unbelievers.*
>
> —LUKE 12:42-46

The moral purpose of this parable (see the context of the above quotation) is apparent. While the steward maintained an attitude of watchfulness, he was faithful and sober; but when he said in his heart, "my lord *delayeth* his coming," he began to beat his fellow servants and to eat and drink and be drunken. Watching for the Lord then is an incentive to loyalty and fidelity, while unwatchfulness results in worldliness of heart, carelessness of walk, and carnality of life.

The return of our Lord is presented as a motive to *brotherly love*: "And the Lord make you to increase and abound in love one toward another, and toward all men, even as we do toward you: to the end he may stablish your hearts unblamable in holiness before God, even our Father, at the coming of our Lord Jesus Christ with all his saints" (1 Thess. 3:12-13). In view of the fact that our Lord may return at any hour, how awful are divisions between the Lord's own people. Soon shall each of us appear before the *Bema* of Christ, where every wrong will be righted and every misunderstanding cleared up. The Lord is at hand; therefore let us put aside our petty differences, forgive one another even as God has for Christ's sake forgiven us, and increase and abound in love one toward another.

The perennial hope of Christ's Second Advent is also used as a call to *a godly walk*: "For the grace of God that bringeth salvation hath appeared to all men, teaching us that, denying ungodliness and worldly lusts, we should live soberly, righteously, and godly, in this present world; looking for that blessed hope, and the glorious appearing of the great God and our Saviour Jesus Christ" (Titus 2:11-13). How clear it is from these words that the Blessed Hope is intended to check the spirit of self-pleasing and self-seeking in the believer and to promote holiness in daily life. As says the apostle John, "Every man that hath this hope in him *purifieth himself*, even as he is pure" (1 John 3:3).

The return of our Lord is also designed to *comfort* bereaved hearts:

> But I would not have you to be ignorant, brethren, concerning them which are asleep, that ye sorrow not, even as others which have no hope. For if we believe that Jesus died and rose again, even so them also which sleep in Jesus will God bring with him. For this we say unto you by the word of the Lord, that we which are alive and remain unto the coming of the Lord shall not prevent [go before] them which are asleep. For the Lord himself shall descend from heaven with a shout, with the voice of the archangel, and with the trump of God: and the dead in Christ shall rise first: then we which are alive and remain shall be caught up together with them in the clouds, to meet the Lord in the air: and so shall we ever be with the Lord. Wherefore comfort one another with these words.
>
> —1 THESS. 4:13-18

Those to whom the apostle was writing were sorrowing over the loss of loved ones. But observe, he does not seek to console by telling them that shortly they would die and join the departed in heaven. No; he held before them the prospect of a returning Savior who would bring back the sleeping saints with Him.

The promise of the Redeemer's return is calculated to develop the grace of *patience*: "Be patient therefore, brethren, unto the coming of the Lord. Behold, the husbandman waiteth for the precious fruit of the earth, and hath long patience for it, until he receive the early and the latter rain. *Be ye also patient; stablish your hearts:* for the coming of the Lord draweth nigh" (Jas. 5:7-8). These words were addressed to saints who were poor in this world's goods and who were groaning beneath the oppression of unrighteous employers. How timely is this word of exhortation to many a twentieth-century saint! How many of God's poor are now crying unto the Lord for deliverance from pecuniary difficulties, from tyranny and injustice! These cries have reached the ears of the Lord of hosts, and just as He intervened of old on behalf of Israel in Egypt, so will He speedily come and remove His people from their present cruel taskmasters. In the meantime, the word is, "Be patient therefore, brethren, unto the coming of the Lord."

The hope of our Lord's return *is the antidote for worry*: "Let your forbearance be known unto all men. The Lord is at hand. *In nothing be anxious*" (Phil. 4:5-6, RV). Brethren in Christ, why be so fearful about meeting next year's liabilities? Why be anxiously scheming and fretting about the future? Why be worrying about the morrow? Tomorrow you may be in heaven. Before tomorrow dawns the assembling shout may be given. At any hour your Savior may come. The Lord is at hand, and His appearing will mean the end of all your trials and troubles. Look not then *at* your dangers and difficulties, but *for* your Redeemer. "In nothing be anxious."

The prospect of a speedily returning Savior is employed to stimulate *sobriety and vigilance*: "Knowing the time, that now it is high time to awake out of sleep: for now is our salvation nearer than when we believed. The night is far spent, the day is at hand: let us therefore cast off the works of darkness, and let us put on the armor of light" (Rom. 13:11-12). The "salvation" here spoken of is that mentioned in Hebrews 9:28 ("Unto them that look for him shall he appear the second time without sin unto salvation"), which salvation is brought to us at Christ's Second Advent. Note particularly that this salvation is not presented as a distant hope, to be realized at some remote period, but is set forth as that which is nigh at hand.

Ere closing this chapter one other question claims our attention—

WHY IS IT THAT OUR LORD HAS TARRIED TILL NOW?

Why has not the Redeemer returned long ere this? At first sight perhaps this inquiry might appear almost irreverent, and some may feel inclined to remind us that "secret things belong unto the Lord." In response we would say, it is not in any spirit of idle curiosity, nor is it to indulge an inquisitive speculation that we take up this question, but simply because we believe that a humble examination of it will prove profitable to our souls, inasmuch as the answer to our inquiry demonstrates the wisdom and grace of Him with whom we have to do.

Of old the mother of Sisera cried concerning her son, "Why is his chariot so long in coming? Why tarry the wheels of his chariot?" (Judg. 5:28). We might well appropriate these words to our present inquiry. On the eve of His death, the Lord Jesus said, "I go to prepare a place for you. And if I go and prepare a place for you, I will come again, and receive you unto myself; that where I am, there ye may be also." But eighteen centuries have run their weary course since then *and He has not yet returned!* Is not this deeply mysterious? A world in which iniquity abounds more and more; an Israel without a home and without a king; a church rent by division and, like Samson, shorn of its power; a groaning creation and a war-stricken earth—all unite in crying with the souls under the altar, "How long, O Lord . . . ?" (Rev. 6:10).

Why then such delay? Why has the millennial era of blessedness been thus postponed? Why has not the Redeemer returned to enter into His blood-bought inheritance long ere this? Stupendous questions surely. Questions that sometime or other exercise the hearts of all the saints of God. Is it possible to discover a satisfactory answer? A *complete* answer, no, for now "we know *in part*." But *an* answer, yes—an answer that will at least enable us *to see*, even though it be "through a glass darkly," something of the *meaning* of our Lord's delay. Why this protracted interval since the time of His departure? Why has He not returned long ere this? We answer—

First, because God would give man full opportunity to develop his schemes and thereby demonstrate the world's need of a competent Ruler. Man cannot complain that God has not allowed him full opportunity to experiment and test his own plans. Man has been permitted to do his utmost in ruling and regenerating the world. God, as it were, has put the reins of government into man's hands and withdrawn for a season. Why? To show whether man was sufficient for these things. To show whether or not man was capable of governing himself. To show whether man was competent to grapple successfully with the powers of evil that war upon his soul.

Throughout the ages man's efforts have been directed toward ruling and regenerating the world. Man has been given full scope. With what results? With the result that the human heart's incurable hatred for God and the utter depravity of human nature have been fully displayed. How has man used the freedom, the opportunities, the privileges, the talents with which his Maker has endowed him? To what profit has he turned them? Have they been used with the purpose of glorifying God or of deifying himself? To ask the question is quite enough. Loud have been man's boasts. Lofty have been his claims. Pretentious his vauntings. Such terms as *improvement*, *advancement*, *enlightenment*, *evolution*, and *civilization* have been his favorite slogans. But the wisdom of this world is foolishness with God, and the folly of the world's wisdom and the vanity of man's claims are now displayed before our eyes. What has "civilization" effected? With all our so-called enlightenment and progress, what have we attained? Let the records of our law courts tell us. Let the columns of the daily newspapers make response. Let the economic political and moral conditions of the day make answer. Let the World War with all its inhumanities, its barbarities, its fiendish atrocities, give reply. And mark, it cannot be said that these things are due to man's ignorance and inexperience. Man is not just starting out to make history. We are now living in the *twentieth century* of the Christian era. Man then cannot complain that God has not given him plenty of time to mature his plans. No; God has given ample time, time enough to show that man is an utter failure, time enough to demonstrate that he is totally incapable of governing himself, time enough to prove that if relief comes at all, it must come from *outside* himself.

Here then is the first part of our answer: Christ's return has been delayed in order to provide opportunity for man's plans to develop fully. *God waits till harvesttime*. He has been waiting for the harvesttime of man's schemes and efforts. He has been waiting patiently with sickle in hand, and as soon as the crops of human industry have fully matured, the word will go forth: "Thrust in thy sickle, and reap; for the time is come for thee to reap; for *the harvest of the earth is ripe*" (Rev. 14:15).

Why has not our Lord returned long ere this? We answer—

Second, in order that God might fully display His long-suffering. "But, beloved, be not ignorant of this one thing, that one day is with the Lord as a thousand years, and a thousand years as one day. The Lord is not slack concerning his promise, as some men count slackness; but is long-suffering to us-ward, *not willing that any should perish*, but that all should come to repentance" (2 Pet. 3:8-9). All through these nineteen centuries the Lord has been saying, "Come unto me, all ye that labor and are heavy laden, and I will give you rest." Ever since the Savior left the earth, God has been dealing with the world in mercy instead of visiting it with judgment. God's patience toward our wicked race has been truly marvelous. Wonderful it is that the vials of His wrath have not been emptied upon the nations long ere this. What long-suffering Jehovah hath shown in bearing with such rebels these twenty centuries! Why is it that the Day of Salvation has lasted until it now exceeds in length every dispensation that has preceded it? Why is it that the door of mercy still stands open wide and God is yet beseeching sinners to be reconciled to Himself? Why is it that Christ has not long, long ago returned in flaming fire to take vengeance on them that know not God and obey not His Gospel? Why is it that He is not even now seated upon the Throne of His Glory and saying to His enemies, "Depart from me, ye cursed, into everlasting fire, prepared for the devil and his angels"? Why? Because the Lord God is "long-suffering to us-ward, not willing that any should perish." Suppose that Christ *had* returned five, ten, twenty, fifty years ago, then, in such case, how many who read those lines rejoicing that they have been accepted in the Beloved would have perished in their sins! Join, then, with the writer in returning thanks for the marvelous long-suffering of our gracious God.

Why has not the Lord returned long ere this? We answer—

Third, in order that God might fully test the faith of His own people. This has ever been His way. Why those years of waiting before Abraham received Isaac? Why that protracted bondage in Egypt, when the chosen people groaned beneath the burdens imposed on them by their cruel taskmasters? Why those four centuries of silence between the ministries of Malachi and John the Baptist? Why a 4,000-year interval from the giving of the promise of the woman's Seed until its realization? Why? To test the faith of His people, to demonstrate the reality of their confidence in Him. So it is in this dispensation as well. Why has our Lord tarried so long in the Father's house? Why these eighteen centuries for His church to journey through the wilderness of the world? Why is it that the first, the second, and the third "watch" have passed and yet our Lord has not come? Why did God permit knowledge of the Blessed Hope to be recovered almost a hundred years ago, and still the Bridegroom tarries? Why this earnest expectation on the part of His own for three generations past and even now the heavens are silent? Why tarry the wheels of His chariot? Why? Because God would fully test the faith of His people. Why is He pleased to do this? To the praise of the glory of His grace. Perhaps to demonstrate to the angels, to whom we are "made a spectacle" (1 Cor. 4:9), that God has a people who by His grace can trust Him even amid the darkness of a profound mystery!

Wonderful are the ways of our God. Scoffers may cry, "Where is the promise of His coming?" Evil servants may exclaim, "My Lord delayeth His coming," and our own wicked hearts may sometimes be tempted to murmur against the long delay. Nevertheless, it shall yet be seen that He "doeth all things well."

GLOSSARY

Amillennialism: The view that the thousand-year reign of Christ described in Revelation 20 is an invisible, spiritual reality rather than a literal earthly kingdom. Amillennialists believe that the kingdom exists right now, and the thousand years is not to be taken literally; so the next event on the prophetic calendar will be the return of Christ, followed immediately by the final judgment.

Antichrist, the (Also see *Beast, the*). The apostle John is the only biblical writer who uses this term, and he uses it only in his epistles. He speaks of "the Antichrist" as a particular individual who was yet to come, but he also recognized that "many antichrists"—people whose opposition to Christ is manifest—had already come into the world.

Beast, the: The creature who arises in Revelation 13:1-10. He becomes a world ruler and a stern persecutor of the people of God (v. 7), as well as an object of worship to the rest of the world (vv. 15-18). He is the ultimate earthly enemy of Christ (19:19), and he is usually identified as "the Antichrist" of 1 John 2:18; 4:3, "the man of sin" and "the son of perdition" from 2 Thessalonians 2:3-4, and "the prince who is to come" in Daniel 9:26.

Bibliology: The branch of theology concerned with the inspiration and authority of Scripture.

Christology: The branch of theology concerned with the person and work of Christ.

Day of the Lord, the: The final outpouring of apocalyptic judgment on the earth (Isa. 13:9-11; Ezek. 30:2-19; Joel 1:15; 2:30-32; 3:14;

Amos 5:18-20; Zeph. 1:14-18; Zech. 14:1-4; Mal. 4:1, 5). The New Testament employs the expression "day of the Lord" at least three times, arguably four (Acts 2:20; 1 Thess. 5:2; 2 Pet. 3:10; and 2 Thess. 2:2 in the oldest manuscripts). The Day of the Lord is sometimes also referred to as "the day of doom" (Job 21:30; Jer. 17:17) or "the day of vengeance" (Isa. 61:2; 63:4; Jer. 46:10). Other New Testament synonyms include "the day of wrath" (Rom. 2:5), "the day of visitation" (1 Pet. 2:12), and "that great day of God Almighty" (Rev. 16:14). In all these contexts, the emphasis is on judgment and "destruction from the Almighty" (Joel 1:15). The Day of the Lord is associated with both Armageddon (Zech. 14:1-4) and the final judgment and destruction of the earth (2 Pet. 3:10), even though the book of Revelation separates these events and places the millennial kingdom between them (Rev. 19:17—21:1).

Eschatology: The branch of theology that deals with future things.

Exegetical: Having to do with *exegesis*, the careful analysis and explanation of a biblical text, especially in the original language.

False Prophet, the: Revelation 13 describes two beasts who arise—the first from the sea (v. 1), and the second from the earth (v. 11). The second beast acts in the capacity of a false prophet. He works great signs and wonders (vv. 13-14), and he causes people to worship the first beast (vv. 12, 14-18). After chapter 13, the apostle John refers to this second beast as "the false prophet" (16:13; 19:20; 20:10), and the first beast is referred to simply as the Beast (see *Antichrist, the; Beast, the*).

Full preterism: A euphemistic label for hyper-preterism (see below). Also called "consistent preterism" and "realized eschatology."

Glorification: The instantaneous completion of the sanctifying process. This is the final aspect of God's saving work for the redeemed (Rom. 8:30). It involves even "the redemption of our body" (v. 23). "This corruptible must put on incorruption, and this mortal must put on immortality. So when this corruptible has put on incorruption, and this mortal has put on immortality, then shall be brought to pass the saying that is written: 'Death is swallowed up in victory'" (1 Cor. 15:53-54). This will occur when Christ returns, and the dead in Christ are raised, and those who are alive and remain are caught up to meet Him in the air (1 Thess. 4:16-17). Glorification means instantaneous Christlikeness for all the saints: "When He is revealed, we shall be like Him" (1 John 3:2).

Hamartiology: The branch of theology that deals with sin.

Hermeneutical: Having to do with the principles by which we interpret Scripture.

Hyper-preterism: The view that *all* prophetic events spoken of in Scripture were fulfilled by A.D. 70. Hyper-preterism echoes the error of Hymenaeus and Philetus, who taught that the Second Coming was already past, thus overthrowing the faith of some (2 Tim. 2:17-18). Hyper-preterists usually spiritualize the meaning of Christ's return, denying that Christ will return in bodily form. They typically try to reconcile that claim with Acts 1:11 ("This same Jesus, who was taken up from you into heaven, will so come in like manner as you saw Him go into heaven") by denying that Christ ascended bodily into heaven. Some even go so far as to deny that He rose bodily from the dead, to avoid having to explain how the Ascension might have been anything other than bodily. So hyper-preterism eventually entails the denial of several cardinal doctrines of Christianity. This view is not the same as *preterism* (see below), though both views are based on a similar misunderstanding of Matthew 24:34 ("This generation will by no means pass away till all these things take place").

Justification: The act of God whereby He declares a believing sinner righteous. This is possible without compromising God's justice because Christ's righteousness is imputed to the justified person. In a similar sense, the sinner's guilt was imputed to Christ at the cross, and Christ fully atoned for it. Thus in justification, the guilt of sin is atoned for through Christ's death, and all the merit of Christ's perfect life is transferred to the sinner.

Millennium, the: The thousand-year earthly reign of Christ described in Revelation 20:1-7.

Olivet Discourse, the: Christ's prophetic discourse recorded in Matthew 24—25 (and abbreviated parallel accounts in Mark 13 and Luke 21). It is an extended reply to His disciples' questions (Matt. 24:3) about the destruction of the temple, the end of the age, and His return.

Partial preterism: See *Preterism*.

Pneumatology: The branch of theology that deals with the Holy Spirit.

Postmillennialism: The view that the church will establish the earthly kingdom of Christ through preaching (and according to some, through political means). Postmillennialists believe Christ will reign over a literal earthly kingdom, but most believe He will do so from a heavenly throne, after which He will return to earth and institute final judgment.

Premillennialism: The view that Christ will return to earth to establish an earthly, millennial kingdom, over which He will reign from an earthly throne.

Preterism: The view that the Tribulation prophecies of Matthew 24 were all fulfilled in the destruction of Jerusalem in A.D. 70. Preterists maintain that Matthew 24:34 ("This generation will by no means pass away till all these things take place") proves that all the prophecies of disaster in the Olivet Discourse were fulfilled in the fall of Jerusalem in A.D. 70. This view should be distinguished from the more extreme view known as hyper-preterism (see above). Unlike hyper-preterism, mainstream preterism does not deny the future bodily return of Christ to earth or the literal resurrection of the dead. The more mainstream variety of preterism is often labeled "partial preterism" by advocates of hyper-preterism.

Rapture, the: From the Latin *rapio*, "to seize, snatch away." This is the coming of Christ in the air *for* His saints (1 Thess. 4:14-17)—as opposed to His coming to earth *with* His saints (Zech. 14:5).

Soteriology: The branch of theology that deals with salvation.

Theology proper: The branch of theology that deals with the doctrine of God.

Tribulation, the: A seven-year period of earthly troubles that immediately precedes Christ's coming in glory. This period is associated with the seventieth week of Daniel's prophecy, during which "the prince who is to come" defiles Jerusalem and the temple of God (Dan. 9:26-27). Premillennialists generally understand the judgments described in Revelation 6—18 as events that take place during the Tribulation. Daniel's "prince" fits the same description as the beast of Revelation 13. There are several other clear parallels between the events described in Revelation and Daniel's prophecy (cf. Dan. 7:25; 12:7; Rev. 12:14).

Type: A symbolic foreshadowing of some truth about Christ (usually employing people or events from the Old Testament to prefigure traits or incidents pertaining to the Messiah). For example, Israel's bondage in Egypt was a graphic foretelling of the infant Christ's retreat from Herod (cf. Hos. 11:1; Matt. 2:13-15), and the bronze serpent raised on a pole in Numbers 21:9 was also a type, representing Christ's crucifixion (John 3:14).

Notes

Introduction

1. Throughout this book, eschatalogical and theological terms that are italicized when they first appear are defined in the glossary at the end. *Hyper-preterism* should be distinguished from *preterism,* though they share a similar hermeneutical approach and would interpret many Bible prophecies the same way. Simple preterism suggests that the "Tribulation" prophecies of Matthew 24 and Revelation were fulfilled in early church history. (Most would say these events occurred in connection with the destruction of Jerusalem by the Roman army in A.D. 70.) *Hyper*-preterism presses the same hermeneutic to a far-fetched extreme (thus justifying the "hyper-" label). Hyper-preterists argue that not just the Tribulation prophecies, but *every* prophetic promise of Scripture has already been fulfilled. (See main text for more details.)

   I strongly disagree with the preterist approach to prophecy, and it is clear that the hermeneutical approach taken by preterists is what laid the foundation for the hyper-preterist error. Nonetheless, the charge that hyper-preterism is a sub-Christian heresy does not necessarily apply to simple preterism. Hyper-preterism's denial of fundamental doctrines such as the literal resurrection of the dead and the bodily return of Christ is what makes that view such serious heresy, not the hermeneutical method per se.

2. Ward Fenley, "The Resurrection of the Dead Already Happened!" (http://www.preterist.net/articles/index.htm).

3. Best-selling author and Christian Reconstructionist David Chilton began to espouse hyper-preterist tenets a few years before his death in 1997. Perhaps partly because of Chilton's influence in the Reconstructionist movement, and partly because the movement has always been warm toward the preterist approach to Bible prophecy, the Christian Reconstructionist movement has shown a particular susceptibility to hyper-preterism.

   Walt Hibbard, founder of the mail-order Christian book service Great Christian Books (GCB), also embraced hyper-preterism and was aggressively peddling hyper-preterist literature in the front pages of his book catalogs before GCB went out of business in early 1999. One of the works Hibbard was promoting most vigorously is hyper-preterism's main manifesto, Ward Fenley's *The Second Coming of Jesus Christ Already Happened* (Sacramento: Kingdom of Sovereign Grace, 1997). Several large hyper-preterist Web sites are now promoting the view via the Internet.

4. Ward Fenley, "Christ's Post-Resurrection Mode" (http://www.preterist.net/articles/index.htm).

5. Ward Fenley, "Psalm 69: The Sins of Christ" (http://www.preterist.net/articles/index.htm). Historic Protestant orthodoxy has long held that our *guilt* was imputed to Christ, and that He paid the penalty for it, suffering the full wrath of God against sin. But we deny that Christ was *made* a sinner in the sense Fenley's remarks suggest. Remember that Christ's righteousness is imputed to believers in precisely the same way as our guilt was imputed to Christ. But we are not thereby automatically *made* righteous. We are justified while we are still sinners (Rom. 4:5). Similarly, Christ bore our guilt without being *made* unrighteous. Fenley's remarks are an affront to Christ, who could never be personally defiled by sin, even while bearing the guilt of multitudes whom He saved (Heb. 7:26).

6. Hal Lindsey, *The Late Great Planet Earth* (Grand Rapids, Mich.: Zondervan, 1970), 53-54.

7. Hal Lindsey, *The 1980s: Countdown to Armageddon* (New York: Bantam, 1980), 12.

8. Ibid., 43.

9. Edgar Whisenant, *88 Reasons Why the Rapture Will Be in 1988* (Nashville: World Bible Society, 1988).

10. Harold Camping, *1994* (New York: Vantage, 1992).

11. I received a letter from one such zealot the very day I began work on this book. He said he had always found my books and tapes to be a blessing, but recently someone informed him I hold a *premillennial* perspective of biblical eschatology, and as a consequence he had completely lost confidence in me as a teacher. He said he had noticed that I often quote approvingly from men like C. H. Spurgeon, Iain Murray, and some of the leading Puritans. And he suggested that if I had really read their works and agreed with these men, I would know that *amillennialism* is the only biblically defensible approach to eschatology. He hinted that my citing these men approvingly without embracing their eschatological views is not entirely honest, and he suggested in the future when I quote them I should consider adding a disclaimer noting that I differ with their eschatological position.

    But in point of fact, these men were *not* amillennialists. Spurgeon was a premillennialist, and Iain Murray is a postmillennialist. Murray's book *The Puritan Hope* suggests that postmillennialism was the predominant view of the Puritans too. I have profited greatly from the writings of all these men, but that does not obligate me to accept every nuance of their theology, nor is a disclaimer necessary when I quote them with agreement. Our differences all involve secondary matters, not things essential to the Christian faith and fellowship.

12. There are several varieties of premillennialism. "Historic premillennialism" and post-tribulationalism virutally eliminate any distinction between the Rapture and the return of Christ, placing both events immediately after the seven-year Tribulation period. The "prewrath" view and midtribulationism suggest that the Rapture will occur during the Tribulation. I hold to pretribulationism, the view that the Rapture occurs before the Tribulation begins. Pretribulationism

is the only variety of premillennialism that preserves the expectation of Christ's imminent appearing discussed in chapter 2. A thorough examination of each variety of premillennialism is far beyond the scope of this book. But many of my exegetical reasons for holding the pretribulational view will be clear as we work through our Lord's Olivet Discourse in chapters 3—10.

Chapter 1: Why Christ Must Return

1. Anthony L. Little, *Faith, Reason, and the Reality of God: A Search for Honesty* (Greenwich, Conn.: Empowerment, 1999), n.p.

2. The primary reference of Hosea 11:1 is to the Old Testament nation of Israel, called out of Egypt. But Israel herself was a prophetic *type* (a symbolic prefiguring) of Christ—and therefore typologically, Israel's sojourn in Egypt prophetically foreshadowed the infant Christ's flight into Egypt. Hosea 11:1 is therefore cited as a prophecy of the infant Christ in Matthew 2:15.

3. In modern times the word *dowry* usually conveys the idea of money or property brought by the bride to her husband at a marriage, but in biblical times the dowry was a gift bestowed by the bridegroom and his family on the bride (cf. Gen. 34:12).

Chapter 2: Is Christ's Coming Imminent?

1. Dennis McKinsey, ed., "Imminence," in *Biblical Errancy*, May 1990.

Chapter 3: Christ's Greatest Prophetic Discourse

1. The disciples' expectation of an immediate, literal earthly kingdom was so deeply ingrained in their thinking that even after Christ rose from the dead, they still expected Him to establish His earthly reign immediately. The last question they asked Him before He ascended to heaven was, "Lord, will You at this time restore the kingdom to Israel?" (Acts 1:6). His death and resurrection had not lessened their anticipation of the earthly kingdom but heightened it. Surely now that He had conquered even death, He would unveil his glory to the world and establish the never-ending kingdom.

   And notice that Jesus' reply in Acts 1 is no rebuke for thinking the kingdom would be a literal, earthly one. In fact, He tacitly affirmed that His kingdom would indeed be established on earth, but not according to *their* timetable: "It is not for you to know times or seasons which the Father has put in His own authority" (v. 7). Thus without dashing their hope of an earthly kingdom He called them to a ready preparedness while they waited for God's timing to be manifest.

2. The Western Wall, which remains standing even today, was part of the retaining wall built when the temple mount was expanded to make room for the immense structure Herod wanted to build. As such, it held up the temple's outer court, but it was not part of the temple building per se; so it is no exception to Christ's prophecy that not one stone of the temple would be left standing.

Chapter 4: Birth Pangs

1. Postmillennialists often argue against premillennialism on the grounds that it is too "pessimistic." (Some even mockingly nickname it "pessimillennialism.") But I deny that premillennialism is pessimistic in any unbiblical sense. It is certainly true that premillennialists are pessimistic with regard to this evil world system, but that is quite a biblical perspective, because there is nothing in this world to be optimistic about (1 John 2:16-17). "Do not marvel, my brethren, if the world hates you" (1 John 3:13). The world despises Christ (John 7:7), and that is precisely why we are chosen and called *out* of the world (John 15:18-19). Scripture clearly indicates that this world's hatred of Christ will not only continue unabated, but will even grow worse—until He personally returns to destroy evil and judge the unrighteous. That, in fact, is the very gist of the Olivet Discourse.

   So with regard to Christ's ultimate triumph over His enemies, premillennialists are more than optimistic. We believe the final triumph will be won easily and instantly by Christ Himself at his appearing. But we do not expect a hostile world to capitulate gradually to His lordship before He returns in glory, nor does Scripture anywhere teach that such a thing will happen. If it seems "pessimistic" to rest our confidence in Christ alone, rather than entertaining the vain hope that the world will become progressively more friendly to Him, so be it. In my assessment, the belief that this world will get better before Christ returns is not "optimism"; it is misplaced faith.

2. Two chronologies have been proposed to show how Daniel's prophecy corresponds to Christ's first advent. The older work is by Sir Robert Anderson, *The Coming Prince* (Grand Rapids, Mich.: Kregel, 1954 reprint). A newer treatment of the subject is Harold Hoener, *Chronological Aspects of the Life of Christ* (Grand Rapids, Mich.: Zondervan, 1977).

3. Notice that all the sealed ones are representatives from the tribes of Israel, again suggesting that during the Tribulation era God's dealings are chiefly with national Israel. The seal indicates ownership, authenticity, and protection.

Chapter 6: Signs in the Sky

1. Revelation 6:12-17 and 8:6-12 describe the same cosmic phenomena.

2. Gary Demar, "The Passing Away of Heaven and Earth" (http://www.preteristarchive.com./PartialPreterism/pp-mt2425.html).

3. Several leading preterists have openly and forcefully condemned hyper-preterism as serious heresy.

4. At a February 1999 Ligonier conference on eschatology in Orlando, the preterist view was strongly promoted by a series of speakers. During the conference, Kenneth Gentry stated that Matthew 24:29-31—including the cosmic signs and Jesus' return in glory in the clouds—was already fulfilled in A.D. 70. Gentry, a preterist whose opposition to *hyper*-preterism is well known, hastened to add that he does not mean to deny that there will be *any* future literal bodily return of Christ to earth. But he also clearly believes Matthew 24 is not the place where a literal Second Coming is taught. A hyper-preterist critic in attendance noted that Gentry did not offer any *other* Scripture references to show where a future

Second Coming *is* taught. Todd D. Dennis, "The Impact of Preterism: Victory in Orlando" (http://www.preteristarchive.com./MinistryUpdate/vr-02-99.html).

Indeed, Gentry's own interpretation of Matthew 24:29-31 effectively eliminates all the major biblical objections to hyper-preterism. If the promise of Christ's return on the clouds in the Olivet Discourse pertains to a spiritual event already past, why not interpret *all* the New Testament references to His return the same way? If Matthew 24:30 is merely a metaphor describing something that took place during the destruction of Jerusalem, doesn't it make perfect sense to interpret *every* biblical mention of Christ's return as a reference to that same already-past event? The obvious dilemma of Gentry's position was not lost on the hyper-preterist critic, who pointed out "that this loudest Second Coming passage in the New Testament is applied [by Gentry] to A.D. 70, with no equal passage being given to assert a post-A.D. 70 coming" (ibid.). Plainly, preterists who allow an allegorical and symbolic interpretation of Christ's most significant Second-Coming prophecy have no credible answer for hyper-preterists who claim *all* the New Testament Second-Coming prophecies are allegorical.

The writer of the above-cited article derided Gentry's conviction that Christ will nonetheless return visibly someday: "Unfortunately, [Gentry] didn't supply any passages which spoke of a third coming" (ibid.). Thus hyper-preterism precisely echoes the scoffers' taunt: "*Where is the promise of His coming?*" (2 Peter 3:4)—and preterism's hermeneutical method simply stokes the skepticism that provokes such scorn.

5. Eusebius, *Church History*, 3:25.

6. Ironically, Kenneth Gentry argues against hyper-preterism by citing Clement of Rome's belief in a future resurrection: "Clement of Rome lived through A.D. 70 and had no idea he was resurrected! He continued to look for a physical resurrection (Clement 50:3 [sic; see rather 24:1-2; 26:1])." If Clement's looking for a future resurrection is so significant to Gentry, why does he not also think it significant that from the first-century church, through the time of the Church Fathers, through the Protestant Reformation, and all the way up to the present day, the overwhelming mass of believers have looked for a future fulfillment of the Olivet Discourse prophecy?

7. This prophecy seems to have had an immediate application to the judgment and destruction of Babylon (vv. 1, 17; cf. Dan. 5:30-31). Yet the full meaning of the prophecy clearly looks beyond Babylon to a yet-future eschatological fulfillment, as evidenced by two things: 1) the cosmic and worldwide catastrophes spoken of in the prophecy itself (vv. 10-13), and 2) Isaiah's reference to the Day of the Lord (v. 6), which is still spoken of as a yet-future reality long after the judgment of Babylon (cf. 2 Pet. 3:10). The only reasonable conclusion is that Isaiah 13 is like many passages of Scripture that deal with both near and far events. And in this case, the near event—the judgment of Babylon—was a kind of microcosm of the final Day-of-the-Lord judgments.

8. I'm aware, of course, that Peter cited this very passage in his Pentecost sermon and implied that verse 28 ("I will pour out My Spirit on all flesh; your sons and your daughters shall prophesy, your old men shall dream dreams, your young

men shall see visions") was fulfilled in some sense by the events at Pentecost. Looking at the broad context of Joel, it is clear that Joel is prophesying about the catastrophes associated with the Day of the Lord (2:1). It is equally clear that the apostle Peter regarded the Day of the Lord as something yet future (2 Pet. 3:10). So Peter could not have been declaring every aspect of Joel's prophecy fulfilled. When he cited this passage at Pentecost, he was obviously making reference to the outpouring of the Spirit in particular, and he probably meant merely that Pentecost was a preview of the Day-of-the-Lord outpouring.

9. This will include Gentile believers as well as Jewish ones. Zechariah 8:23 says, "In those days ten men from every language of the nations shall grasp the sleeve of a Jewish man, saying, 'Let us go with you, for we have heard that God is with you.'"

Chapter 7: Does Anybody Really Know What Time It Is?

1. Christ's omniscience was one of those aspects of deity, like His eternal glory and His omnipresence, that was temporarily veiled by the humanity He took on Himself. As we noted in the Introduction to this book, our Lord did not dispossess Himself of any of the divine attributes, but He took on a fully human nature. In other words, His incarnation involved the addition of a human nature, not the subtraction of any aspect of deity. But He was *fully* human in every sense. Hebrews 2:17 says, "In all things He had to be made like His brethren," and that meant the conscious knowledge in Christ's human mind was such that He could genuinely and truthfully say, in His humanity, that He did not know the time of His own return. In a different sense, and in His omniscient divine mind, He certainly did know, because He knows all things (John 16:30).

2. Matthew Henry, *Matthew Henry's Commentary on the Bible* (Old Tappan, N.J.: Revell, n.d.), n.p.

Chapter 9: The Tragedy of Wasted Opportunity

1. It is even more similar to the parable of the minas in Luke 19:11-27. The lessons and many of the main details are identical, but the parable of the minas and the parable of the talents differ in some of their secondary details and were clearly given on different occasions.

2. Our word *talent*, used to speak of natural abilities, is derived from the imagery of this parable.

Chapter 10: The Judgment of the Sheep and Goats

1. This would explain how the earth is populated in the kingdom. Children born to these people during the thousand years would therefore need redemption. Perhaps that is why at the end of the millennial kingdom, when Satan is released for a little while, there will still be people susceptible to his deception (Rev. 20:3). After he is released, he will even be able to garner followers for one last futile rebellion (vv. 7-9).

Appendix: The Imminent Return of the Redeemer

1. This appendix is excerpted from Arthur W. Pink, *The Redeemer's Return* (Swengel, Penn.: Bible Truth Depot, 1918), 157-181.

2. The above Scripture refers primarily to our Lord's return to the earth, as is evident from the fact that here He styles Himself "the Son of Man"; yet, like all prophecy, it has at least a *double* bearing and therefore may be properly applied to His secret coming in the air. (All Scripture references in this appendix are from the King James Version of the Bible.)

3. A sentinel's challenge ("Who goes there?")—i.e., we are to be on the alert.

SCRIPTURE INDEX

General Index